Feng Shui For Lovers

Sarah Bartlett is a trained astrologer and tarot reader with many celebrity clients, and frequently broadcasts on TV and radio in this capacity. She is the author of several books including The Love Sign series and *The Love Tarot*. Sarah Bartlett lives in a small village near Saffron Walden.

FENG SHUI
for Lovers

How to create harmony and energy
in the spaces of your heart and home

SARAH BARTLETT

Kodansha International
New York • Tokyo • London

Kodansha America, Inc.
114 Fifth Avenue, New York, New York 10011, U.S.A.

Kodansha International Ltd.
17-14 Otowa 1-chome, Bunkyo-ku, Tokyo 112-8652, Japan

Published in 1999 by Kodansha America, Inc.

Originally published in 1997 by Vista.

Library of Congress Cataloging-in-Publication Data is available

ISBN 1-56836-271-4

Manufactured in the United States of America

99 00 01 02 03   QFF   10 9 8 7 6 5 4 3 2 1

To All Who Seek Harmony in the Universe

Contents

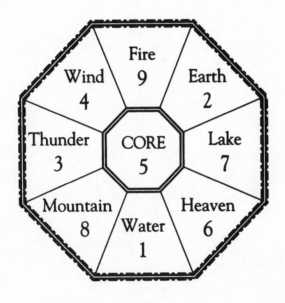

The Bagua

Preface

When I was a child I was taught to believe in God, but God didn't quite get the hang of who I was, so I gave up on Him and joined the Cosmic Dance instead.

Many years ago, when I lived in Malaysia as a skinny adolescent, I met a fascinating and remarkable Chinese lady who lived next door. Lim had a talent for something that she called 'magic', and which many years later I found out was known as Feng Shui.

Her son and I used to go fishing in the storm-drains after the humid rains, or play Mah Jong in the shade of the verandah. Lim was one of those mothers who was not only a friend and guide but also an *inspiratrice* – someone who told you secrets and magic.

I was introduced to Feng Shui when the flying ants arrived on a visit. One evening we sat building Mah Jong walls on the green baize table out on the verandah. Flying ants came in swarms when the nights were sultry and still. Most folk shut their doors and flicked off the lights, but Lim had a different way of dealing with the ants.

'You want to play Mah Jong? Then I make sure ants don't bother you.' She turned off all the lights except for the one above the verandah steps, then fetched a large bowl of water. She placed the bowl on the floor exactly below the lamp. The flying ants swarmed towards us, but mysteriously parted like a tidal wave around the front of the verandah as they came in sight of the light. The dazzling lamp would normally lure them in a frenzy towards our table, but it was as if the reflections that danced on the water in the bowl dazzled them in a different way. For over half an hour the swarm swept past the bungalow without coming anywhere near the light. And then they were gone. 'There, we can turn on the lights again.'

'Why did they come?' I asked stupidly.

'They come on the Ch'i. The Ch'i carries many things, but if you know how to use this magic then you will always be safe.'

'Which magic?'

'The magic of the dance of life. Tomorrow, I show you. You learn about the Red Bird and the Secret Arrows. OK?'

I nodded. This magic sounded just the kind I wanted to learn!

Before You Begin

This book is a guide to using some of the principles of Feng Shui for your own enjoyment and happiness. However, before you start making changes, adding cures and re-organizing your home, it is essential that you read the whole book. The creative application of Feng Shui is a highly complex and skilled art, and it takes many years to become an accomplished Feng Shui practitioner.

Don't expect instant results. If you pick up the book, dip into a chapter and implement a cure without knowing why, you will be doomed to disappointment.

Feng Shui is a journey and this book takes you on that journey. It shows you how to open pathways and gradually introduce changes to harmonize your life. Miracles have been known to happen but the secure way to a harmonious life-style is to take your time. Give your home, and yourself, space and time for the energy to find its own level of harmony.

Just like the ancient Feng Shui masters who would sit for weeks in the valley to understand the true energy of the valley, and sit for hours on the mountain peaks to know the true energy of the mountains, the magic will start to work only if you have learned to become a part of it yourself.

Introduction

Feng Shui (pronounced 'Foong Shway') is the Chinese art of placement. Feng means Wind and Shui Water. The ancient Chinese believed that man, living creatures, the world and everything in it were connected by the flow of universal energy. What the Wind and Water did was tell you which kinds of energy were running through the mountains or the landscape. The Wind was Yang, active, dynamic energy, and the Water was Yin, passive, receptive energy. It was the simple channelling of these two forces in nature that became Feng Shui to the ancient Chinese mystics. Even contemporary scientists now agree that the whole universe vibrates and interconnects via a force or energy. In the art of Feng Shui this energy is called Ch'i.

For centuries, many Eastern cultures have relied on the complicated art and science of Feng Shui in carefully planning the site of houses, offices, paths, gardens and interiors to create and achieve balance and harmony. Over 3000 years ago the Taoists used Feng Shui not only to decide which were the most auspicious locations for their ancestors' tombs but also to enrich their sexual energy. The key to long life and happiness was to be found through enhancing the flow of Ch'i during love-making.

The same principle that Ch'i flows through everything, from the mountains and trees to the furniture in your room, is still used in contemporary Feng Shui. This energy is a powerful and almost magical force and most practitioners believe that Ch'i must be used not for personal gain but for the good of everyone. So when our homes and gardens are mapped out according to Feng Shui principles, the energy will flow through our back garden, through our hearts and into everyone else's back gardens and hearts too.

Feng Shui is a complex subject and it takes many years of study and training before you can become a practitioner. There are several different schools of Feng Shui. One is based on the more classical and scientific approach which uses a detailed and powerful compass, plus astrology and astronomy; another, a subtle blend of intuition and spiritual awareness. There is also a school which concentrates simply on cures and enhancements.

This book shows you how to try out some of the simpler principles of this exceptionally organized system, and how to add a touch of magic to your emotional and sexual lifestyle.

The magic of Feng Shui is that the changes you make and create in your home enable the energy to work *within yourself*.

Feng Shui in the home and heart

By creating and changing the spaces in your home, you can begin to enhance your energy for both physical and emotional well-being.

Getting the environment right is a means of getting

yourself and your relationships right. You have a heart and so does your home! The heart of your home is something you must locate. For example, flopping out in front of the TV may seem a cosy option, but it might be worth exploring other places in your home to check if the TV and the sofa are really where love, warmth and happiness can be found. Balancing and harmonizing the place where you express your *self* is a way of achieving the same harmony in your relationships.

What Feng Shui does is look at what is going on *now*, right under your nose and under your bed. It is about adding objects, colours, scents and plants, moving furniture and getting rid of clutter; creating new spaces in your environment, repositioning beds, using water, candles, wood, fabrics, mirrors, crystals, lighting, gadgets and your own inspiration to enhance the sexual and emotional energy between you and your lover. After all, if the bedroom is in harmony with *you*, then the energy that it invokes will enrich your sex life.

So what has Feng Shui got to do with relationships?

There are many kinds of relationships. This book is mostly concerned with love relationships because love is often elusive and difficult to understand. Love follows its own paths of energy within us; from one day to the next it can alter our hearts and kidnap our feelings. You know what it's like to wake up one morning and feel you're in love. And you know what it's like to feel emptiness, when a lover leaves or you just can't stand the relationship any more. Maybe you get rid of the grief by painting your home, having a good springclean or making more of a mess. Maybe the clutter gets worse when you fall in love. The washing never gets done, and the fridge looks more like the inside of a dustbin. We put into our surroundings what is going on inside us, both emotionally and in our spirit. This is our own personal Ch'i. We all try to be individual, separate and detached from one another and from the natural world. But however much we try to fight against losing our individuality, we're part of the earth and the universe and there's no escaping it. So we should enjoy and nurture ourselves, and it too.

As human beings we relate not only to our partners or lovers, but to the world and all the vibrations and energies around us. We aren't often aware of this, but *relating* is exactly what we do with the environment every moment of our existence. Sometimes this relating becomes more obvious, for instance, when we step outside the house on a freezing cold morning; or when we get tangled up with highly energetic intimacy between the sheets! Even Einstein's theory of relativity labours the same point.

A cat instinctively knows how to relate to the world. When a cat gets lost it finds its way home by walking round in an ever-increasing spiral until it reaches the energy field it knows as its territory (see Figure 1). This energy, this spiral, is Ch'i – a path, a channel and always a *connection*. If you follow this path you'll never miss home! In Chapter 11 you will find out how to use this cat spiral yourself.

Feng Shui is about the balance of energy within our spirits, our hearts and our minds as well as in our surroundings. We *are* the Ch'i; we carry our own energy and draw it in from everyone else and give some back too. Relationships are about two people (or more if you're in a love triangle,

Figure 1: Cat spiral.

enjoy lots of relationships at the same time or live in a commune) and that means there's more harmony and balance to sort out than when there's just you. Your home, whether it's a bedsit, a mansion or a semi in the suburbs, is a reflection of your personal tastes and the fashions of the day. But your home is also a mirror of the *inner you*; an expression of your life and love, whether there's a clutter of clothes and books in every room, or a perfect symmetry of colour co-ordination and neat and tidy tables.

Getting it right

Feng Shui can be a lifelong study and practice. But this introductory guide lets you into a few tips and secrets that you can use straight away for more harmonious relationships. The energy we create, or the energy that is already inherent in the environment, is something we can modify, change and improve to enhance our lives and our love and bring us more in touch with who we really are and want to be.

Feng Shui is a major component of Chinese astrology. Your destiny and your lifestyle reflect the energy of your inner being. By using the key Feng Shui elements which express your personal energy, you can bring love back into your life, or create harmony for you and your lover.

When do you use Feng Shui? There might be something missing in your relationship, or maybe it's just going through a bad patch. Your partner may have left you; or you're single and trying to find the ideal lover. You may have to create a special space, or totally springclean the house; welcome new objects or colours or ideas or qualities into your home to enliven a stale relationship. To enjoy sexual harmony you might have to hang a crystal in your window or move the bed. Simple elements and simple organization. Don't forget: As above, so below. As without, so within. The environment you create is at the same time the journey you take towards successful relationships.

Chapter One

The Bagua

There are two mysterious keys to Feng Shui. The first is the Bagua. (Most people agree this is pronounced 'Baagwa' but it is sometimes spelt Pa-Kua.) The second key is the elemental energy of Chinese astrology, which is determined by the year of your birth. The five elements are Fire, Earth, Metal, Water and Wood. There's a special element-year table on page 64 which tells you which one you are. But first let's look at the Bagua, your instant map for finding out where to change things in your home, and which areas of your relationships and your self need harmonizing.

The Bagua represents the invisible patterns of energy in anything from a whole landscape, a city or an office block to a house, a room, a garden, a human being and even a relationship. By using this ancient grid system we can see which areas of our house may need attention, and consequently which areas of our relationships can be enhanced and vitalized. This is the map we use to determine what's going on where in the spaces of your home and heart.

The Bagua is based on a magic number square as shown in Figure 2.

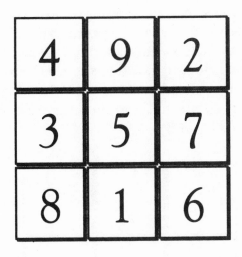

Figure 2: magic number square.

This magic number square is an ancient Chinese system that has mystical powers. It is believed that about 4000 years ago a tortoise emerged from a river carrying on its back special markings which the Chinese interpreted as the numbers one to nine – our primary numbers. Even Western mathematicians like Pythagoras got excited about the magic square and realized numbers were extremely potent symbols. Whichever way you add up the lines of the square, the total is fifteen. In the West this number isn't significant, but in the East it is considered magical and powerful.

Traditionally, the Chinese relied on the fifteen-day cycle between the New and Full Moon to mark the twenty-four phases of their solar year. The Chinese, incidentally, have many different time cycles, but this one is eminently auspicious!

Each of the nine numbers corresponds to an *invisible*

energy that has specific meaning in your love life. This pattern of invisible energy moves through everything. So the Bagua reflects both the energies within you and your relationships, and the energies within your home. Each of these numbers is represented by a key word. For example, the number 1 area relates to Water, the number 2 to Earth and so on. Look at Figure 3.

Wind 4	Fire 9	Earth 2
Thunder 3	CORE 5	Lake 7
Mountain 8	Water 1	Heaven 6

Figure 3: The magic square becomes the Bagua.

The central section of the square represents *oneness* or *completeness*. So number 5, the middle number, is the heart of the home, the essence of you, the key to your relationship, and it is called the Core.

The nine Bagua energies

Each section of the Bagua has its key word and, most importantly, its special connection with areas of your relationships and your sex life. Here is the list:

The Bagua energies and their love connections

1	Water	Beginnings, new romance, freedom, flow
2	Earth	Receptivity, feelings, intuition
3	Thunder	Family, outside influences, intrusions
4	Wind	Harmony, happiness, progression
5	The Core	Life energy: Are you in touch with *you*?
6	Heaven	Give and take, emotional support, friends
7	Lake	Sensuality, senses, sexuality, creative love
8	Mountain	Awareness of self or other, communication
9	Fire	Clarity, fulfilment: Are you in tune with each other?

What we do when we create space, move things round our house, bring in new objects or clear old ones out, is essentially what we are doing on a different level within our spirit. (To some people, using the word 'spirit' might imply spiritualists and psychics, the afterlife or other-worldliness. What I'm referring to is the primeval energy that is within us all.) We each have a spirit which is our vitality; an energy which drives us on like an inner voice we cannot hear. It is this which connects us with the invisible energy or Ch'i.

What we are going to try to do is to encourage good and auspicious energy into our homes and into our love lives, and keep less favourable energy away, or use it and transform it creatively. By placing mirrors, statues, plants or crystals

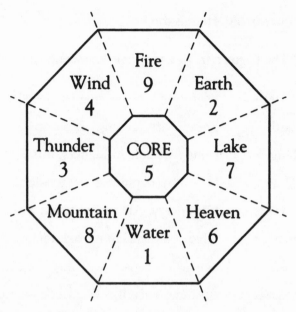

Figure 3A: The magic square becomes the Bagua.

around our house we are in a sense placing their qualities within our spirits too. This is what Feng Shui is all about. For the energy within is also the energy without.

Using the Bagua

Now you've seen the shape of the Bagua, the first thing you have to do is to copy Figure 3A on to a thin sheet of tracing paper, then draw yourself a plan of your room or house or wherever you live. It's important to determine which is your front door. You may have a back door that you yourself use more than the front door, but your front door is still the one which you open to guests, to strangers, to the outside world. This is the most crucial entry point of the Ch'i energy into your home and the starting point for your journey. If you live in a flat or bedsit, have a room in your parents' house or anything unusual, then you should choose the door that *you* open to let in the big wide world – friends, the postman, strangers, creatures from outer space. The Bagua can be used for specific rooms as well as whole houses. For example, bedrooms always play a crucial part in our sexual relationships so placing a Bagua map over the bedroom might illuminate what is going on specifically in your sex life.

Next, place the Bagua over the plan you've drawn, as shown in Figures 4 and 5. If you've got a square or symmetrical room or house this will be easy. But if you've got bits sticking out, extensions or odd-shaped rooms, then find the centre by drawing two diagonal lines and place the core of

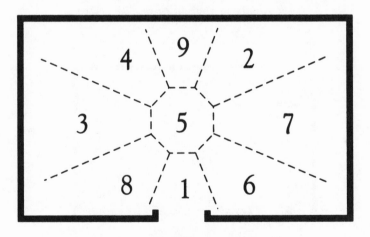

Main
Entrance

Figure 4: Placing the Bagua.
A regularly shaped house or room.

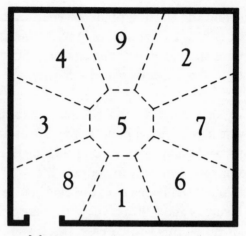

Main
Entrance

Figure 5: Placing the Bagua.
A regularly shaped house or room.

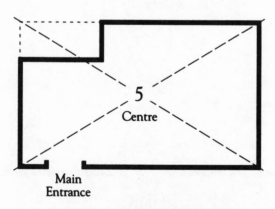

Main
Entrance

Figure 6: Placing the Bagua.
To find the centre of an irregularly shaped room or house,
square off the missing areas to make an imaginary regular
shape and draw two diagonal lines from the corners.

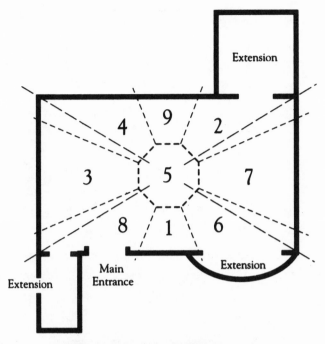

Figure 7: A house with extensions.
These extensions will form projections of the Bagua area.
They adjoin to make these areas more powerful.

the Bagua over it and the bottom line – 8 1 6 – on a level with your front door (as in Figure 6). You may have to contract or extend the Bagua to fit in with rectangular or unusually shaped rooms. You can now see in which areas of your house or room the invisible energies are located.

Look at the spaces that appear to have no energy in them. For instance, in Figure 8 a large section of number 7, Lake, is missing. These spaces will show you which particular Bagua energies might be missing in your home. Their lack will be reflected in your relationships and they can be encouraged back by a simple cure if need be.

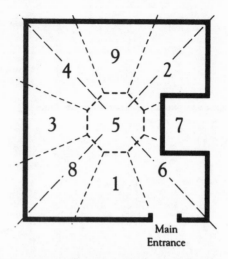

Figure 8: A house where the extensions have created a missing space. Here the Bagua area 7 falls mostly outside the house.

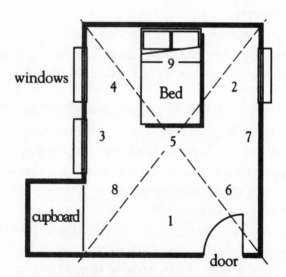

Figure 9: A bedroom Bagua.
The cupboard here is a projection of 8 – Mountain.

28

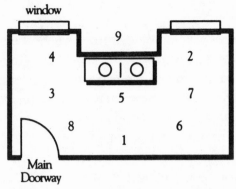

Figure 10: A kitchen Bagua. Here most of 9 and some of 8 are missing.

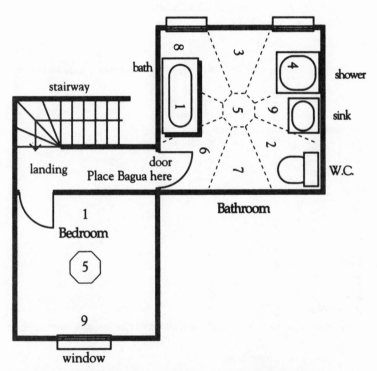

Figure 11: A bedroom and bathroom Bagua. Always use the doorway of a room to align the Bagua.

Any area of your home or room where there is a surge of energy – where an awkward-shaped room juts into or through the Bagua space in a particularly powerful way – is also highly revealing. These energies are enhanced, so you can see which areas of your relationship or your own inner needs are most successful or volatile.

Figure 12 is a diagram of Jane's house. Jane consulted me because she was having great problems with her in-laws who were always interfering in her relationships. On the plan, the area of the Bagua energy relating to in-laws, inheritance and outside influences (number 3, Thunder) is in the kitchen. We therefore focused on her kitchen first. I noticed that her

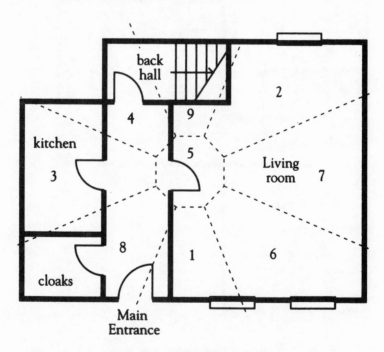

Figure 12: Plan of Jane's house.

stove and her sink were right next to each other. In traditional Feng Shui this is not auspicious because there is nothing to bridge the two conflicting types of energy: one hot and fiery, the other wet and watery. After standing a wooden jug between the sink and the stove to create a bridge, Jane found that her in-laws soon became less intrusive in her life.

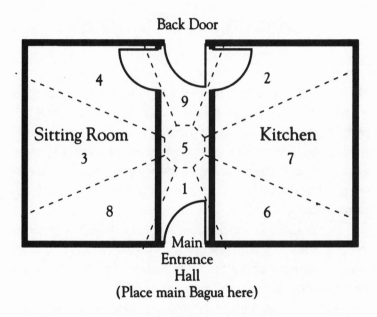

Back Door

Sitting Room

Kitchen

Main
Entrance
Hall
(Place main Bagua here)

Figure 13: If there is more than one entrance, place the Bagua on the one you open mostly to guests.

Chapter Two

Opening the Pathway

Now you know which part of your home corresponds to which part of the Bagua, follow the guide below to open the pathways for beneficial and vitalizing energy to flow through your life and home. You can open whichever one of the pathways you feel is the most important for you *now*. Or you can open more than one, or open them as and when they become important to you.

Crystals and semi-precious stones are highly auspicious in Feng Shui. They are not particularly expensive, and even a small fragment of crystal holds more energy than you can ever imagine. If you can't find the specific stone or crystal mentioned, then use the alternative suggestion until you discover the right piece.

Always place crystals where they can reflect and catch the natural light. This doesn't have to be on a window ledge, but make sure your crystal is not surrounded by clutter. The vibrations work better if the crystal is placed on a table, ledge or shelf with no other objects nearby. If the Bagua area overlaps two rooms, place the crystal in the room you use most. Finally, don't ever clean your crystals with polish. Rinse them in sea water if you can. If you live in the middle of a city then wash them briefly in mineral water.

1 Romance

To open the pathway for a new romance or a more flowing relationship, place either Rose Quartz, Pink Tourmaline or Pink Kunzite in the area of your home that corresponds to the Water area of the Bagua. If you can't get hold of these crystals, place a pink candle in a glass candleholder. Make sure you light it at least once a week.

2 Feelings

If you want to open the pathway that leads to being in touch with your feelings and more emotionally aware of the feelings of others, place Smoky Quartz or a Moonstone in the Earth area of your home. If you haven't access to these stones, place a deep smoky black candle in a glass candleholder and light it regularly.

3 Intrusions

To help to clear the pathway of outside influences so that you can be sure you are making your own choices, place a piece of Aquamarine or Sodolite in the Thunder area of your home. If you can't find these crystals, place an aquamarine or bluey-green candle in this area instead.

4 Harmony and trust

To ensure harmonious progress in your relationships and to open the pathway to trusting that journey, place Yellow Citrine or Topaz in the Wind area of your home. If these are not available, use yellow candles.

5 Wisdom, understanding your own values

To open the pathway to greater wisdom and insight in your love life place Amethyst crystals or a piece of Lapis Lazuli in the Core area of your home. If you can't get hold of these, place deep purple or deep blue candles in this area instead.

6 Friends, give and take, support

To open the pathway to honesty and the value of friendship in your love life place Malachite or Green Tourmaline in the Heaven area of your home. Use deep green candles and light them regularly if you can't get hold of these crystals.

7 Sensuality, creative and sexual love

To ensure the pathway is open for expressive and enriching sexual love, place Carnelian, Garnet or Bloodstone in the Lake area of your home. If you can't find these, use dark ruby red candles and make sure you light them frequently.

8 Communication

To open the pathway for good communication in either your physical or emotional relationships, place Turquoise or Amazonite in the Mountain area of your home. Again, if these are not available use turquoise-coloured candles in clear glass candlesticks.

9 Clarity for self: Are you in tune with your partner?

To ensure the pathway is open to enable you to know what

you truly want in love, or to be really in tune with your partner, place either a Diamond, Selenite or Clear Quartz crystal in the Fire area of your home. If you can't get hold of any of these, use pure white candles.

Once you have decided which (it can be more than one) of these pathways to open, Chapter 3 will explain more about the energy you are working with.

Chapter Three
The Bagua Energy Profiles

All the Bagua energies are important and you may find that you move through them at different stages, whether you're in a relationship or are single.

1 Water
Freedom, flow, new romance, beginnings

We cannot survive on this planet without water. Water nourishes and sustains, and yet it can also be one of the most powerful and dangerous forces for human beings to attempt to control. The oceans are moved by both the Moon and the Earth's gravity. These powerful forces of nature also energize the seas, rivers and lakes. Rivers must flow to the sea, and our weather systems are governed by the currents of the air so that we get storms, rainclouds, monsoons and blizzards. The energy of Water is always moving, fluid, changing direction and often making new courses.

In traditional Feng Shui, Water was always Yin energy. At times fluid and elusive; at other times stagnant in ponds and puddles. Water dragons were auspicious symbols of prosperity and moral goodness. In Feng Shui, water dragons were believed to be the carriers of Ch'i and could be found in meandering streams as well as the sky. A water dragon always prefers the curves and spirals of river courses and rainclouds to the straight lines and angles of viaducts or man-made canals. The early Chinese mystics believed Water had its own strength: a gentle strength, soft and passionless. But Water was also to be feared and admired when it took the form of torrents or raging streams and waterfalls. Water was often seen as a symbol of how wealthy you were. If a river or a stream gushes fast in a straight line from your house, then so does your money! Don't live over a watermill or near a dam.

Water is one of the most powerful energies of the Feng Shui principle. It symbolizes the flow and the freedom in our Bagua. Water in your relationships or love life is about introducing a flow, setting something in motion. Perhaps you are embarking on a new romance or going through a difficult patch when neither of you is communicating. Maybe you're desperate to meet up with someone again or a new colleague looks promising but you're not ready to take the plunge and risk making a fool of yourself. Perhaps you've just bumped into someone in the street and that urge to keep going back to the same place in the hope of meeting them again is beginning to wear you down. You might want to find some freedom within yourself, or to open up a conversation; to be frank and honest about your feelings; to instil confidence and to bring about self-awareness of where you are going in your love life.

Water is about getting relationships to move forward. Maybe things have got stagnant and you're stuck in a rut. If you want to push your partner into a commitment, you might need to pay attention to this area in your house and your heart to see whether freedom could be a problem. If you are feeling trapped, too committed, don't want to make promises, then perhaps rearranging this area of your house or bedroom could prove restorative.

Water can symbolize choosing a new direction in your relationship. Perhaps you want to cool things down, be less involved and more free to do your own thing. You might even need to end it.

Water also relates to your sexual energy, as does the Lake section. Is making love a voyage of discovery and adventure, or is it a boring half-hour you've squeezed in between the ten o'clock news and bedtime? Are you getting the freedom to explore new ways of love-making, or does your partner insist on the same old routine?

If sexual energy isn't flowing, go to this area of your home and place a piece of Rose Quartz there. However, if love-making is a bigger problem, you may need to look at the creative love (Lake) section of the Bagua as well, particularly the Bagua area of your bedroom – and even the bed itself.

2 Earth
Receptivity, feelings, intuition

Water flows and we go with the flow or not as the case may be. But the Earth is where we live. Where we feel safe and grounded. It is also our nourisher, for without the Earth we would have no oceans, no rivers, no rain, no water. Earth is symbolic of our awareness of ourselves as separate from the universe. It allows us to understand that we are from the universe. It allows us to understand that we are individuals. As babies we discover we are not part of our mother, not safe in a womb-like state of non-awareness. While we are in touch with our bodies we are in touch with our feelings. We begin to know fear. In traditional Feng Shui, the Earth symbol is Mother Earth, Yin, and all things female.

When we lose contact with the Earth, we lose contact with our feelings, with our intuition and our receptivity – in other words, our ability to take in what is being given out from the world, from nature, from our partners, from our lovers. If we are in touch with the Earth, we are better able to receive and ultimately to give. Jung once said that man believed himself to be an 'unfinished creature'. And that's exactly what most of us are, acting as if there is something out there to find, a meaning in life, or another relationship which will solve our problems and produce instant happiness. Most of us do this through our relationships. And that is why Earth is such an important invisible energy to work with.

Some of us live through our emotional responses, while others refuse even to acknowledge we have feelings. If this is the case this area of the Bagua might be missing in your house. You may believe you are out of touch with 'feeling', or that others are demanding too much from you, when you'd rather shrug your shoulders and just get on with doing your own thing. When we avoid responsibility for our lives we refuse to admit that others have their own values and needs. Sometimes denying we have feelings can lead us into stormy waters. Earth needs to be put into the context not just of our own feelings but also the feelings of others.

This area of the Bagua might need attention when you're getting over-emotional, too intense, too possessive, too angry. It might also need attention if you can't express your emotions easily, or you feel hurt, betrayed or left out in the cold.

You may feel that no one can relate to you emotionally, that all your partner wants is sex, or fun, or to remain aloof and non-involved. Alternatively it may be you who projects coldness, and it may be worth investigating whether emotion is difficult in your relationships. Perhaps feeling is something you prefer to close the door on, just like a room full of junk or a cupboard that gets so full you can't even open the door any more for fear of the whole lot spilling out. Emotions can get pushed into cupboards too. And the fear of opening emotional cupboards is alarming to some of us. Earth is a crucial area of energy that needs careful balancing.

3 Thunder
Outside influences, family, intrusions

We all know what Thunder sounds like. And we all have an inkling of how it is created in the sky. And yet although Thunder can scare us, reminding us that nature is not beholden to man, it still arouses and excites us. Some people hide under the stairs or stuff their heads between pillows. Others open the doors and windows and gaze longingly at the extraordinary power of the universe. But Thunder is also subtle, and can be upon us before we even know it is there. Thunder plays a big part in our weather systems. The energy is powerful, for Thunder brings lightning and rain.

Disconnected from Earth we view Thunder as a threat, as an alien. Yet we have created it ourselves. In many ways our egos are like the Thunder in the sky. For our Thunder has moved far away from being at one with the Earth so that we are aware only of our immediate selves, and we rarely hear it coming before it's too late. Many animals know a storm is on its way a long time before it arrives. They sense it on the wind, or in the Ch'i. We have lost that instinctive knowledge. And that's why we don't know who or what is coming into our lives or our relationships to stir things up, to influence us or, more importantly, who it is who is undermining us.

So you might say Thunder is about intruders. Not necessarily malignant ones, but influences from outside our environment which unbalance us, incite us and shake us up until we are not sure if it is us who needs to change or something out there which we can't quite put our finger on. Usually it's both. Thunder is about the beginning of a cycle, of birth and fertilization. But symbolically this is also the fertilization of new influences, of subtle undercurrents in your own life and your relationships. External inspiration or external intrusion.

The people who do this best, often without being aware that they are doing it, are our family and sometimes our friends. Although there is a separate section for true friendship (number 6, Heaven), it is worth bearing in mind when you look at the Thunder area of the Bagua whether there are some who may not be as true to you or your relationship as they appear. Thunder moves around unseen. It can make a lot of noise – it may rage through your life in the guise of your well-meaning mother-in-law or friendly flatmate – but

41

it works undercover. This is not to say that these people are maliciously trying to destroy your relationship, but the results of their unconscious behaviour can be deep and wounding.

Some people get a kick out of playing Thunder games. They may usually be well-meaning and supportive but they get hooked on trying to influence and change your life because they daren't even look at their own. So the intentions of others are like Thunder. It wants to control, it wants to roar through your life and incite you into actions or emotions that are not yours but theirs. It is all their feelings projected on to you. But it can have a big and sometimes disastrous effect on your life and relationships.

For example, like my client Jane you might find that your in-laws are forever on your doorstep interfering with your marriage. One of the most painful influences is when a parent or friend tries to live their own life through you. In a way you become their shadow – their little project – so that all the goals they might aspire to are ultimately directed into you as their vessel of intent. As this is often done unconsciously, particularly by parents, you may never realize it until some major crisis or change in your relationship brings Thunder clapping and banging into your bedroom. Thunder brings with it dark clouds and usually rain. This is where your sex life may need an umbrella.

Parents sometimes expect their children to go out and do the things they wish they had done. Empty regrets and sacrifices made for love, children or family are projected on to offspring by martyred mothers and fathers. By instigating changes in your home in this area of the Bagua you can begin to recreate your own influence on yourself, which in turn can enable intruders or muck-stirrers to realize you have a life of your own. Then they may accept that your relationship is your problem, not theirs.

4 Wind
Harmony, happiness, negotiation, progress

Wind is the Feng in Feng Shui. In ancient Babylon and Egypt the Wind was known to be a carrier of the breath of life, while Water was the bringer of the source of life.

In many civilizations and cultures the Wind is known as the Spirit. Some of these spirits are good and some bad. In traditional Feng Shui you would avoid building a house or your ancestors' tomb on the top of a hill because you would be exposed to too many wild winds. On the other hand, if you live in an area where not even a breeze can flow through your window you're also asking for trouble. Stagnant Ch'i is as bad as wild Ch'i. Nowadays it's still advisable not to sleep above an empty garage or storeroom as there may be much stagnant and perhaps unhelpful energy below you.

Wind symbolizes harmony, progress and happiness. But our friend the Wind can be both calming and moving yet highly dangerous. Hurricanes cause destruction and death, yet traditionally the gentle breeze is the carrier of good luck and happiness.

Harmonious energy is carried on the Wind, and when you feel the breath of Ch'i on your face as the breeze passes you by you will recognize the uplifting power of this energy. This is auspicious Ch'i, the kind of energy you want in your house and in your heart. Our friend the Wind carries the clouds that make the rain, that bring Water – Shui. Wind is also connected to Wood, to the branches of a tree gently swaying in the wind, yet attached to the Earth and therefore safe, nourished and grounded. This is where Wind symbolizes penetration and progress. For without progress – a subtle and gentle movement forward within a relationship – there can be no harmony. A still Wind makes for a static relationship.

When we look at this area of the Bagua in our homes and hearts we have to consider how still the relationship is. Perhaps we have reached a point which seems harmonious and contented, but is it too static? Alternatively we may find the storms and rages of a hurricane in our relationship – tempestuous rows, disharmony all around, fights, things getting blown out of all proportion. Lovers may come and go, in and out of our lives without a word, not unlike a wind that gusts through the garden one day, disturbing the leaves but not drying the washing on the line. Wind is powerfully created from those around us, as well as from within us.

Perhaps your partner never seems happy, is always moody, distant, in a grump. Life may be either too intense or too dull. Happiness seems elusive, and often an illusion. The Wind may be blowing quietly through your heart, but not your partner's. Perhaps your relationship never seems to progress, is never transformed, never achieves moments of clarity. Wind could be taken literally as penetration, relating to your sex life and how moving it is. You may find that by creating changes in this area of your home you will suddenly feel a breath of fresh air passing through your life and your relationship.

Wind is also about money and the happiness it can bring or take away from a relationship. Money is one of the biggest sources of conflict within our partnerships. During the first flames of attraction and physical desire you never even think about who's got how much in the bank. Romance takes our attention away from the practicalities of life. But later on in our relationships we begin to think harder about security, and the energy that money and all it represents can bring into our life. Is money static in your relationship, or is it moving well?

Wind carries the breath of life, don't forget. You need to make sure that the Wind area of your home is harmonious first, before you can expect to achieve happiness within yourself.

5 Core
Life energy: Are you in touch with you?

The Core is number 5 and the centre of our Bagua. This is the most profound link in the web, the key harmonic of the invisible energy. The energy here is perhaps the most difficult to deal with and the most obscure to define. Yet it is, at the same time, the most potent and inspirational if you handle it right.

The Core is about being at one with ourselves. In our bodies this area of energy is manifest at a midpoint between our navel and our crotch. In Eastern cultures this is an important centre of gravity – particularly in spiritual body and movement schools like Tai Ch'i and Kitaiso. In these traditions it is called the Hara. It is where our energy starts, the very centre of our being. To us in the West it can be confusing to think that this point below our navel is the source of all our energy and vitality.

In intimate relationships we often believe that being in love is the pinnacle of life, the moment we have been waiting for and which will never end. But being in love is a temporary illusion and the feeling of euphoria usually wears off with time. Those of us who throw ourselves into many different relationships are often doing so because we get a buzz out of being 'in love'. This is because we assume that being 'in love' is what love is all about. We may not know how to love ourselves. Real happiness lies within us, not outside.

Your Core can help you discover who you really are and what love is. To be in touch with ourselves is one of the hardest lessons we have to study in life. Some of us never see who we really are. It is only disastrous love affairs, broken marriages, divorce or our own boredom that begin to give us an inkling of what is going on beneath our desires.

Number 5 unifies all the other areas of the Bagua. When we make changes here we must be careful about our motives, because wanting to change things to gain personal power or to pursue selfish desires will affect all areas of the Bagua and all areas of our relationships. The consequences of changes here are crucial.

But our life energy often needs to be activated. We may be out of touch with ourselves and blind to what is going on around us. For if you cannot see yourself, you cannot possibly understand what is going on for everyone else. If your relationship has just fallen apart for any reason, look carefully at the location of this area of the Bagua in your home.

Is your Core a key inspiration in your heart and home? If it's situated over the toilet, think about where all that life energy is disappearing. If your Core is in the hallway, use a cure to prevent the Ch'i from rushing out of the front door and taking your Core energy along with it. For example, place a mirror next to the entrance door to redirect the energy back in. Life energy needs to flow, but it has to be a two-way traffic.

6 Heaven
Give and take, emotional support, friends

Heaven is where we start to open up to others, to begin to nourish the things outside ourselves and to recognize that 'them out there' and 'me in here' can relate on a level where there is harmony and acceptance of each other. Once we travel on past the Core, we begin to put relationships into a new framework, whereby it is not just me who is doing the relating. Everything in the universe is relating in a unique way. This is where we begin to sense the underlying invisible energy that connects all things. Like a child growing up, first we must leave the safety of the womb, then we go through another phase of leaving home; we may even have to give up our roots and our homeland entirely to find out where we are going and how we can get there.

Heaven is male, Yang energy. It *does*. Heaven activates and it looks outside of self. It starts to learn to give and also to take without judgement, without compromise and unconditionally. In traditional Feng Shui, Heaven is the beginning of creation; it is that which comes to Earth to create life.

Symbolic of male energy, Heaven is at the opposite end of the balance to Earth, female energy. Earth is about how we receive, how we feel and how we react to others. The emotions are ours, personal and intuitive. Heaven is about how we express this and direct it, what we can offer, whether we have the givingness and the selflessness. Heaven also reflects the encouragement and return of feelings freely given by others.

This area of the Bagua may need attention if you're always feeling let down, or that others don't trust you, or you can't trust someone else. There may be a conflict of intent in your relationship. Perhaps your partner wants emotional support and you have to do all the giving. Maybe you have a million acquaintances but no true friends. There may be no one with whom you can share your worries or fears. Alternatively you may be the taker and your partner a giver. Somewhere along the line there is inequality.

You may find you never have time for your friends. Perhaps you can't offer them emotional support because your own life is so troubled and unhappy. Maybe there are changes needed in this part of your house and heart? If this area of the Bagua is actually missing in your home, by introducing cures you could find that friends become more supportive of your troubles, and your own needs become less pressing and merge into genuine expansive compassion. (See Chapter 12 on 'Something Missing' for help.) This is not to say we should all be saints – but what we give out is a mirror of the qualities we attract in return.

Our sexual balance may also be in need of improvement. You may feel used, abused even. Perhaps you demand too much sex? This is where both Heaven and Lake need to be investigated together. If your relationships are purely sexual or physically motivated, again this area may be in need of attention or just a good springclean to activate more friendship in the relationship. A partnership that is empty of friendship or true support may not last long. If you feel that you are doomed to merely physical attraction, and that the kind of people who come into your life and your heart always turn out to be different from what you had imagined, look at what is happening in your Heaven. Being attentive to Heaven can instigate a sense of what it is you are projecting that brings them into your life.

7 Lake
Creative love, sexuality, sensuality, stimulation

Physical love is the most potent, magical and inspiring kind of creativity you can perform without having to study or pass exams.

Human nature being what it is, we all have need of sexual experience for one reason or another. But paradoxically 'reason' doesn't come into it at all. The pull of physical attraction is a powerful and mysterious energy. Even scientists have a difficult time when they try to analyse it. Maybe we should just enjoy it for what it is because that magnetic, compulsive quality that brings about ecstatic sexual union doesn't always last for ever. But don't forget what this energy can do in our lives. As well as forming lifetime relationships it can also destroy them. While mysteriously setting off hormones so that couples get together, have children and live happily ever after, it can also provoke some of us into dangerous territory. When we meet someone with the right chemistry, we may embark on the most magical journey or we may climb aboard a rollercoaster to hell and back.

Lake is about the energy of a relationship that becomes itself an almost separate entity. The ancient Feng Shui masters believed that through sexual intercourse one could obtain immortality. Similarly, Tantric sex is a practice where pure orgasmic energy and ecstasy once attained can lead to mystical awareness. Sexual union is powerful, and we must understand it as such.

A Lake is a vast area of still Water. It reflects Heaven and sits happily on the Earth. But Lakes can dry up without rain or without stimulation, and they get covered in weeds and mud. This is a bit like sexual relationships. All that physical attraction that was turning you both on for months or even years may suddenly evaporate. Perhaps it is a mutual drought, or it could be just one of you who changes.

Lake symbolizes the kind of joy you experience when you're deeply 'in love'. It also symbolizes the ability to be creative with one another so that the Lake won't dry up. The downside of Lake is that it symbolizes sexual temptation and/or sexual rejection. If you are always attracted to the wrong type, this is the area of the Bagua which could help you to start meeting the right ones. But you may have to invoke cures in every other area of the Bagua as well if this is becoming a pattern that repeats itself.

Perhaps you are going through a separation or a terrible

love triangle; there may be someone you just can't get enough of, but who is already locked into an intense relationship themselves; it could be a simple case of having met someone new and you want to get your sex life steaming; or you've been with the same lover for years and need to ignite a spark of passion in your life. Whatever the sexual need, problem, physical attraction, discouragement or creative vision you have in mind, this area of your home may need attention. The Lake area of your bedroom and your bed could be other sources of inspiration.

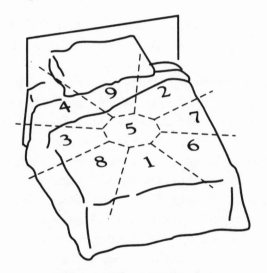

Figure 14: The bed Bagua.

On the subject of sensuality: this is not the same as sexuality. To be aware of your senses, to feel, to touch, to see, to hear, to speak – these are all ways we can increase our physical dimension so as to get in tune with our own and our partner's needs. This area of the Bagua can be harmonized

51

in conjunction with Fire to enhance not only our sexual awareness but our sensuality too. In Chapter 16 on the five elements you can find out the physical and sensual pleasures that relate to you and your partner. Lake is probably the area of the Bagua that responds most rapidly to attention.

8 Mountain
Communication, awareness of self or other

If you ever get a chance to visit one of the greatest mountain ranges in the world such as the Andes, the Himalayas, the Rockies or the Alps, you'll know what kind of energy is involved when you first catch sight of these awesome beasts. It's no wonder the Chinese were fascinated by their extraordinary mountainous landscapes. Mountains give off a surge of power that cannot be described, only felt.

Mountains have always been used in Chinese art as a symbol of that powerful energy, of the dragon veins (channels of energy) that run through great mountainous regions, so that Yang vitalizes the Yin earth. Mountain is neither Yin nor Yang, but is the point where the two opposites can at last become equal. There's a saying, 'as old as the hills', which in a sense reveals how magical the landscape and particularly the bits that stick up into the sky are to us. Mountains are like wise old people; they've been around for years and you can relax with them, enjoying their wisdom without feeling threatened.

Why do we want to climb to the top of a Mountain? What is it we want to prove? The powerful imagery that a

Mountain suggests to us is that of a boundary. When we encounter an obstacle in our way most of us want to overcome it, rather than find an easy way round. Challenge is important if we want to maintain a sense of direction and purpose in our lives. So mountains must be climbed.

In a sense, Mountain is what we must face from outside our own feelings. It involves how we function in relation to another individual. When we begin to accept that other people have their own scars and wounds and defences, we begin to see the boundaries and limitations we impose on ourselves and attract into our lives.

The Mountain makes you stop and think. This is what we need to do occasionally in relationships. Sometimes of course an external event or encounter occurs which forces us to do so. Suddenly we are aware that there is you and me and a Mountain, and we may each have to tackle it our own way. In relationships we often assume we are right, imagine we can climb any Mountain, but find that we have to accept that others have their own pinnacles to face.

Making comparisons is a way of communicating, but rather than making value judgements we have to remember that the way in which I perceive that Mountain, that boundary, may be totally different from the way you perceive it. It's the same Mountain but with two different mountaineers trying to climb it.

In an intimate relationship two people will often communicate but never really listen; they will talk but never speak the truth; they will over-compensate for each other, but never realize they are doing so; and they will never be aware of who it is they are relating to.

You may need to look at this area of the Bagua in your

home if you find you are always having to make compromises in your relationship. Maybe you have no emotional boundaries and are always finding yourself drawn into someone else's feeling zone. Perhaps you are unsure of your own feelings or your own values. Maybe you can't communicate with your partner, or they are not interested in seeing you as you really are.

Alternatively you may feel that you cannot climb a Mountain – that you'll never reach someone. Perhaps you cannot express yourself openly, or feel that a partnership of any kind is beyond your limits.

If you have a Mountain area missing from your home then it may be necessary to re-evaluate your own self-esteem. Do you have feelings of self-worth? Hanging a mirror on a wall to extend the Bagua into a pretend Mountain area may increase your own value of yourself.

Communication is one of the most powerful skills we possess as human beings, but for most of us it brings with it pain and suffering. Learning to harmonize this area of our lives and home can help us to understand that our relationships are made up of powerful energies. However much you are convinced you know your partner, you can never really know another human being. It takes a lifetime to get to know yourself. Harmonizing this area of your life can improve the way you communicate and the way in which you see me in here and you in there, and begin to accept the differences.

9 Fire
Clarity, inspiration: Are you in tune with each other?

Fire has been a potent symbol of energy in every civilization and every religion. Prometheus stole the Fire that Zeus had kept for the Gods to give it to mankind. In mythology it is Fire which gives us our inspiration.

Fire is about the spirit inside us which carries us forward into the future. Without Fire we would have neither insight nor the ability to form a concept and make it into a vision. Without direction and a goal for the future, we stagnate and lose our sense of purpose.

The Chinese considered the Fire-bird a vital source of magic. The area in front of your house is called the Red Bird (Figure 15), a highly auspicious area relating to the energy that needs to be harmonized before it enters your home.

Red has always been a colour associated with Fire, and the Chinese use it frequently in areas of life where money needs to be made and success assured. Fire also represents and connects with the south, an auspicious direction for your front door to be facing. The ancient Taoist character 'Ch'i' symbolized 'no fire'. The paradox here is that without the burning fires of desire and longing to which we attach ourselves, we can at last achieve harmony and oneness – real Fire.

If you feel that the rest of your relationship is going well, but perhaps you need to inspire your sex life or generally improve your vision as a partnership, then Fire may be an area that needs some changes. Getting in tune with each other can almost be a telepathic link if you so desire it. This

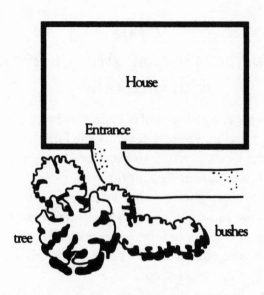

Figure 15: The Red Bird area in front of your house is highly auspicious.

is a way of turning your relationship into a stronger and more lasting connection. However, don't just rush straight to that area of your home and expect your whole love life suddenly to take on a new meaning. Becoming fulfilled and expressing so much positive energy all the time can be exhausting. Remember to give each other space. Use this area of the house as an inspiration to the future for you alone, as well as for any joint ventures.

If this area of the Bagua is not in an accessible part of your house, or if it is missing altogether, you may find difficulty in asserting yourself in a relationship. Perhaps you always feel you have to please someone else. You may lack confidence and be wary of expressing yourself and your ideas. You may find others assume you are being bloody minded and stubborn, when in fact you fear change. If you have more than enough of this area in your home, you could find you are popular, inspiring and full of spirit. Although this is a positive and enjoyable way of living your relationships, you may need to check that you don't get too inflated with a sense of your own importance.

Chapter Four

Getting Rid of the Baggage

After opening the pathways for positive energy to enter our homes and hearts, it is essential to clear out any clutter and mess. You may have already placed your crystal in your chosen pathway, but you should still declutter your home before you start to use more specific cures.

We often have cupboards full of junk and drawers of clothes we never wear. Sometimes boxes of clothes and books sit waiting for the day when we can be bothered to visit the Oxfam shop or get down to the car-boot sale. Layers of dust descend and encourage us to ignore the clutter rather than confront it. This is the same with the emotional baggage we carry around with us from every broken love affair or relationship that didn't turn out to be eternal bliss.

The simplicity of the Bagua energies is that if you clear out your rooms and your cupboard spaces and get rid of the physical mess, this acts as a tonic or a heart cleanser. What you do out there in your home is at the same time being done within your heart and spirit.

Here is a guide for clearing out the dead wood and getting ready to put cures and remedies in the area of the

Bagua you have decided is in need of transformation. By the way, if you have already walked around your house and felt intuitively which part of the Bagua grid is crying out for balance, then make sure you relate it to your feelings, relationship and *current situation*, before steaming in with the vacuum cleaner and the black bags. Understanding what you are doing is as essential as doing it.

As you clear up, think about the things around you (apart from essential items like the bed and the loo brush) and ask yourself what it is they do for you. Do they make you feel angry, hot, cold, dull, excited, inspired, bored, reluctant, enchanted or happy? If they generate positive qualities then keep them, but if your response is negative then chuck them in the bin. Obviously without the negative side we wouldn't have a positive side and if we were surrounded only by positive things this would not necessarily produce harmony. But the energy of you is reflected by the energy of those very things in your room that make up the baggage. If you've stuffed a million so-called 'treasures' into a cupboard, think about whether they really are treasures any more. They may have been once . . . rather like that relationship you treasured eighteen months ago, but you wouldn't cross the street for now!

Mop or mope?

Two approaches to this. One involves dusters, vacuums and spit and polish, the other is a more spiritual ritual, but equally healing.

I'm sure you don't need an explanation of how to turn your vacuum on, or how to polish the furniture. But the art of this kind of purification is not to cheat! Don't just run the duster along the top of the bookcase and pretend that the bits under the vases or beneath the pile of papers don't need polish because you can't see them. That's like avoiding relationship problems because if no one else can see the dust then neither can you. But you always know it's there. Making an effort to clean thoroughly is remarkably cleansing in itself.

Again, with paintings, mirrors, kitchen equipment, floors (yes, behind those sofas too) and anything which you might normally choose to forget, this time choose to remember. If you come across anything that gives you the feeling that it shouldn't be there as it serves no purpose, chuck it out. However difficult that may seem at the time, once it's in the dustbin it's remarkable how quickly you will forget you ever possessed it. Possessions are a reminder of the kind of person you are, so the more knick-knacks and junk you hoard the more likely it is that you need to reassess your values. What is it you look for in a relationship? What are your priorities? Equally someone who lives in a minimalist cell might need to ask: Do my values incorporate the needs of others? Is there something missing from my life?

You may be perfectly content to live in white emptiness or a clutter of objets d'art – whatever suits your style and your taste. But make sure you know, deep inside your heart, that this is a reflection of yourself and that it is not just fashion or someone else (Thunder) dictating how you should look, live and love. Who you are and how you are, are about as obvious to others as a heap of dirty socks or a perfectly ironed pile of knickers. But often it is we ourselves who haven't the faintest clue as to how others perceive us or who we really are.

I was once asked to give advice to a friend of mine, a successful musician. He lived alone, drank like a fish and generally found it difficult to keep any relationship going for more than a few months. He was talented, physically attractive (a subjective statement perhaps, but let's say he found it easy to attract women if he so desired, and not just because he was successful) and now in his late thirties. It wasn't that he was a womanizer. He wanted a permanent relationship desperately, but all the women he met seemed to leave him fairly quickly.

He lived in a Victorian terrace house in a south London suburb. Done up, good vibes, and smelling of old wooden floors, guitars and incense ashes in the fireplace . . . on the surface it seemed harmonious enough. But what stood out from this aesthetic bliss were the endless photos, old letters, videos with 'To Luke, love Jane', and memorabilia of all his ex-girlfriends. Photos at gigs, photos on beaches, Luke and Sue, Luke and Emma, Luke and the world. Great for Luke to live with his memories but not much fun for anyone new to the nest! I began to feel sorry for Luke. He was his own worst enemy.

Although he dreamed of permanence, love and stability, at the same time he clung to that old sentimental sludge. His collection of mementoes was the worst kind of warning to any woman who might have the notion of commitment in her heart.

I gently advised him to take the photos down and put them in an album or stash them in a box in the attic, like most people do. He shrugged his shoulders. The memories were all he had. How could he let go of everything that had meaning in his life? But he'd give it some thought. He was beginning to understand what I was talking about and he'd try to work it out for himself.

A few weeks later I heard through the grapevine that Luke had a new girlfriend. One night I asked her how things were at Luke's place. She said, 'He's got a great house, beautiful guitars, antiques, everything like that. But, you know, I don't think there's much point getting involved. I mean, he's plastered his loo with pictures of his past lovers. Can you imagine sitting there in the morning staring at all those women who've shared his bed? No way!' Well, at least he'd moved all the photos into one room. He had made a start!

Removing clutter may involve chucking out things to which you are still attached. This doesn't mean you have to burn your love letters and photos, or live in a sterile environment with only the smell of Jif to greet you when you return home from work. It simply means dumping off the flotsam and jetsam. We carry an awful load of emotional baggage and if, like Luke, you display it to the world so literally, albeit as a brave and honest pronouncement of your life and loves, there aren't too many of us who will be brave and honest enough to accept it. After all, we've got our own luggage to carry too!

Chapter Five

The Elements and Creating Welcoming Spaces

With the clutter gone and the house sparkling, it's time to perform a few little rituals just to let your home and its energies know that you have cleared out all the dross and are ready to harmonize and organize your life the way you want it.

The best kind of rituals are personal ones that you invent. These can be based on your favourite smells, music or images. Most rituals used traditionally to clear spaces were an integral part of ceremonies and religious invocations and involved incense or another form of 'smoking out'. My advice is, don't get elaborate unless you're an elaborate kind of person. It doesn't matter what you do in the way of a ritual, as long as it feels right to you.

The Five Elements

First, if you haven't already done so, look at the chart on page 64 and find out which element you were born under.

You can then work with your own special energy. (The influence of Yin and Yang will be explained later, on page 199.)

In Chinese astrology, the five elements – Fire, Earth, Wood, Water and Metal – are reflective of different energies in our environment and in us. Harmony is achieved by enhancing the qualities of your specific birth element energy. In other words, the cures you use should be either reinforcements of your own inner potential or ones that seek to balance or enhance energies that may be missing.

Figure 16: Element Years.

Metal Yang	Water Yang	Wood Yang
31.1.00–18.1.01	8.2.02–28.1.03	16.2.04–3.2.05
10.2.10–29.1.11	18.2.12–5.2.13	26.1.14–13.2.15
20.2.20–7.2.21	28.1.22–15.2.23	5.2.24–24.1.25
30.1.30–16.2.31	6.2.32–25.1.33	14.2.34–3.2.35
8.2.40–26.1.41	15.2.42–4.2.43	25.1.44–13.2.45
17.2.50–5.2.51	27.1.52–13.2.53	3.2.54–23.1.55
28.1.60–14.2.61	5.2.62–24.1.63	13.2.64–1.2.65
6.2.70–26.1.71	16.1.72–2.2.73	23.1.74–10.2.75
16.2.80–4.2.81	25.1.82–12.2.83	2.2.84–19.2.85
27.1.90–14.1.91	4.1.92–22.1.93	10.2.94–30.1.95

Metal Yin	Water Yin	Wood Yin
19.1.01–7.2.02	29.1.03–15.2.04	4.2.05–24.1.06
30.1.11–17.2.12	6.2.13–25.1.14	14.2.15–2.2.16
8.2.21–27.1.22	16.2.23–4.2.24	25.1.25–12.2.26
17.2.31–5.2.32	26.1.33–13.2.34	4.2.35–23.1.36
27.1.41–14.2.42	5.2.43–24.1.44	14.2.45–1.2.46
6.2.51–26.1.52	14.2.53–2.2.54	24.1.55–11.2.56
15.2.61–4.2.62	25.1.63–12.2.64	2.2.65–20.1.66
27.1.71–15.1.72	3.2.73–22.1.74	11.2.75–30.1.76
5.2.81–24.1.82	13.2.83–1.2.84	20.2.85–8.2.86
15.2.91–3.2.92	23.1.93–9.2.94	31.1.95–18.2.96

Fire Yang	Earth Yang
25.1.06–12.2.07	2.2.08–21.1.09
3.2.16–22.1.17	11.2.18–31.1.19
13.2.26–1.2.27	23.1.28–9.2.29
24.1.36–10.2.37	31.1.38–18.2.39
2.2.46–21.1.47	10.2.48–28.1.49
12.2.56–30.1.57	18.2.58–7.2.59
21.1.66–8.2.67	30.1.68–16.2.69
31.1.76–17.2.77	7.2.78–27.1.79
9.2.86–28.1.87	17.2.88–5.2.89
19.2.96–7.2.97	28.1.98–5.2.99

Fire Yin	Earth Yin
13.2.07–1.2.08	22.1.09–9.2.10
23.1.17–10.2.18	1.2.19–19.2.20
2.2.27–22.1.28	10.2.29–29.1.30
11.2.37–30.1.38	19.2.39–7.2.40
22.1.47–9.2.48	29.1.49–16.2.50
31.1.57–17.2.58	8.2.59–27.1.60
9.2.67–29.1.68	17.2.69–5.2.70
18.2.77–6.2.78	28.1.79–15.2.80
29.1.87–16.2.88	6.2.89–26.1.90
8.2.97–27.1.98	6.2.99–27.1.2000

1 Fire Element

Your inner energy is potent and passionate

Light those wonderful perfumed candles in the room you are cleansing or cook a delicious meal in your kitchen and let the whole house draw on the aroma. Burn some exotic incense – sandalwood or musky smells are best, especially if you want to create a mood for the room you are about to Feng Shui. Smoke cleanses the atmosphere and drives out the negative energy. (But cigarette smoke doesn't!) Candles can reconnect vibrations and set up a new atmosphere that is reflective of you. Again, use coloured candles that are specifically suited to your needs: white ones for clarification, red ones for passion, blue ones for feeling, green for friendship, yellow for communication.

2 Wood Element
Your inner energy is airy and poised

When I was a child I was given an old bird-of-paradise nest by the lady who taught me about Feng Shui in Malaysia. Every time we cooked a special meal we would tie the nest to the end of a piece of twine and whirl it round and round in the air to drive away the Sh'a Ch'i or bad energy. The noise it made was like the whistling wind, and it was a powerful spell. The chances are you don't have a bird's nest hanging around your kitchen, but try breaking off some dead branches from a tree in your garden or lifting your broom and sweeping the energy in the air inside your home, like sweeping the cobwebs from the ceiling, to stir and disperse any that are rotten. Another way is to move your hands with open fingers through the air – if you feel any resistance push it away or kick with bare feet.

3 Earth Element
Your inner energy is grounded and earthy

This is a good element if you like the simple things in life. Sit cross-legged on the floor and sing your favourite song. The placement of crystals (the ones you like best) on the window ledges and one in the centre of the room can bring healing. Leave them in the room overnight or during the day while you get on with essentials like sleeping or going to work.

This may sound a bit cranky, but you may prefer to write a letter to the room and tell it that the changes you are about to make are functional as well as spiritual. The energy needs to be channelled for the benefit of you, the house and the world. Once you've read your letter aloud in the room, burn it in grand ceremonial style.

4 Water Element
Your inner energy is intuitive and adaptable

Touch all the objects in the room that you want to keep. Give them a name as you do so and make them feel wanted and loved. This kind of emotional contact with inanimate objects may seem soppy, but we have to remember that we are only another projection of the universe and no greater or smaller than anything else in it. Living things are just living things, and all those objects in your room that aren't 'living' in the sense we are, have a life of their own and ought to be respected for their essence. Many of them will have been made from things that were once living, so bow your head to the wooden table and chairs or walk barefoot across the rush mat in the hall.

5 Metal Element
Your inner energy is cool and single-minded

The fifth element and one that's hard to integrate into our Western heads is Metal. To the Chinese, gold and silver were the main associations of this element. Make some tiny silver balls out of crumpled-up aluminium foil or paper, and place them in a metal container in the centre of the room to invoke your personal Metal energy and clear the atmosphere.

Or, if you've got any gold or silver jewellery, place it in a triangular layout beneath the window, or hang your silver trinkets in the doorway. Metal is about friction too, so strike matches and blow out the flame, maybe even try a few indoor fireworks to clear the air.

In performing integrating rituals and using your own special magic you are beginning to explore Feng Shui. By doing these things, in a sense you're preparing yourself and your home for what is to come. You are also getting rid of wasteful energies, old patterns, and setting yourself the challenge of making improvements in yourself and your relationships.

If you feel you need a special place, one which is private and personal, there is no better way than to create a permanent 'magic element corner' of your room. This will play a long-term part in harmonizing your love life. Depending on which birth element you are, creating a Fire, Wood, Earth, Water or Metal display on a small table can extend the cleansing and ritual process for as long as you feel you may need it.

Every time you feel negative, go to that place and remind yourself of your element and your connection to it with love. Also remember to make contact with your magic corner in the real world. For example, if you're Earth, you need to commune with nature; if you're Water, visit the sea or a fast flowing river; if you're Metal, keep a talisman of real gold; if you're Wood, visit a museum, or enjoy the hustle and bustle of the city; and if you're Fire, burn some incense or watch the glowing embers of a bonfire.

Here are some ways of creating magic element corners in a special room. The bedroom is probably best for this as it is less disturbed by intrusive energies from the outside.

Magic element corners to vitalize your inner energy

For Fire

Use a low surface and ensure that it is in the south corner of your room. Place a small mirror at the back of the table against the wall, and set a single red candle or incense stick in front of the mirror. If you have a piece of Carnelian or Bloodstone, place this next to the candle. Use a crimson or deep orange cloth beneath these objects. Find a tiny print or painting of poppies, sunflowers or a red sunset to hang above the mirror; for extra impact place a prism in your magic corner to refract every particle of light.

For Earth

Make sure you choose the north-east or south-west corner of your room. Use a fairly high surface if you can, almost at shoulder height, and place a bonsai tree or a small picture of a Japanese landscape to the rear. Make sure the surface is covered with an old fabric, like a paisley shawl or a piece of faded tapestry. Find a small terracotta bowl and fill it with pebbles or shells you have picked up on the beach. When you have finished your favourite perfume, place the scent bottle in the corner too. You may want to add a piece of Smoky Quartz or a Moonstone.

For Wood

A magic corner for Wood is better at floor level. Make sure you use the east or south-east corner of your room. Cover the area with green baize or a deep green velvety fabric. Place a wooden sculpture of a bird or, if possible, a green dragon (you can find these now in some oriental interior shops). Hang a carved wooden-framed mirror or picture on the wall. If you have one, place an antique book against the corner, and a small fern-leaved plant to one side. Use a piece of Malachite as a centrepiece.

For Water

Use the north corner of your room if you can and try to ensure the surface is at about knee height. Cover it with silk or voile in violet, viridian or Prussian blue. Hang a picture of the sea or a photo of a waterfall on the wall. Look out for fragments of glass or pottery found on the seashore and place them in a small glass vessel in the centre. Alternatively, use a glass bowl full of marbles. Find a stone cup, fill it with water and sprinkle it with glitter; place a piece of Amber or Turquoise at the front for love connection.

For Metal

Make sure your magic corner is in the west or north-west corner of your room. Hang a framed mirror or, if you can find one, a bronze-effect mirror sconce on the wall, and make sure the surface is at about waist height. Place a silver, pewter or metallic vessel – even an old tin that you've cleaned out – in front of the mirror, or use a glass that you've painted gold. If you have a silver necklace hang this from the wall sconce, and include a gilt-framed photo or picture in your corner. Place a Diamond, Selenite or White Quartz crystal in the centre.

Magic spaces

Even if you live in the tiniest bedsit or share a room with someone else, you can make a 'magic space'. In this way, if you are alone, you can welcome new love or invite good flowing energy into your home for better relationships. This magic space is like a waiting room at the station, a place that allows all who travel to take a rest. Your magic space is the waiting room for new lovers, new friends and new partners in your life.

Create your magic space in the area of your home that relates to the Water area of the Bagua. Usually this will be near a front door, a hallway or an entrance. The magic space must be outlined in the air with your finger, as if you were tracing out a square, rectangle, triangle or circle – whichever shape you prefer. Sadly, we can do this only in one dimension, but imagine that you are doing it in a million dimensions at once! When you have decided which portion of the room is your waiting room, purify it with your own element ritual as described earlier; alternatively, place a piece of White Quartz crystal in any area of the room for a day and a night to charge the atmosphere with beneficial energy.

Every time you walk through this area, remind yourself that it is a welcoming space, either for those who physically enter your home or for those whom you would love to enter your life but who haven't yet found the pathway to the space in your heart.

To confirm this area as your magic space, either copy the talisman in Figure 17 on to a piece of paper and hang it on the wall next to your magic space, or actually paint it on to the wall as large as you can. This is an ancient Chinese talisman for combining peace with good fortune, and is an excellent way of vitalizing your home and welcoming love into your life. It also ensures that any uneasy or difficult energy that enters your home is deflected.

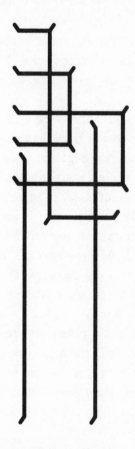

Figure 17: A talisman combining peace with good fortune.

Chapter Six

How to Bring Love into Your Life

This book is not just aimed at those who have partners or lovers or long-term friendships, it's also for those of us who may have just split up, been single for months, perhaps years, and anyone who is lonely and in need of a friendship, partner or lover.

As human beings we need to relate to each other on whatever level has significance for us. We each perceive the world from a different place. If we could begin to realize that we are all part of one universe and not separate, it might be easier to accept that the beast within ourselves is the same beast that is in everyone else. Someone once said that 'every person we meet is a signpost to self-discovery'. That discovery goes beyond our own personal needs and enters the hearts and homes of everyone else on this planet.

There is no right or wrong way to love someone. It's just that sometimes love locks into possessiveness or physical desire and then we don't know what it is any more. When you're out on your own looking for love, you'll often grab it whichever way it comes.

Feng Shui can help you to get a sense of who you really are, and what it is you mean by love in your life. The greatest relationship you can have in life is with yourself. How can you ever love another unique person if you cannot love your own unique self? Getting your house shipshape is the umbilical cord that can connect you to knowing yourself, loving yourself and attracting others into your life who can love you too. Understanding your own needs and values is the way forward to a healthy ego.

Here are some questions you could ask yourself.

1 What am I looking for?
2 Do I have a problem attracting someone?
3 Do I have a problem keeping a relationship going?
4 Do I always seem to go for the wrong types?
5 Why did I split up with my ex-lover?
6 Why can't I stop thinking about X?

The following cures are specifically related to the above six questions. You may want to instigate them all – but don't overload your home all at once or you may confuse your own needs and desires. Use the most important one for you *now* and then the others if and when you change, or your situation changes. If you've already opened the pathway for better harmony in your relationships, doing these cures can take you further down the road.

The kind of love that is important to you now may well change in time, but Feng Shui is flexible. It can move with you, just as love alters its own course.

1 What am I looking for?
This can be a difficult question to ask yourself, and

extremely awkward to answer! If you have problems knowing what you want out of a relationship, or what kind of partner would provide you with what you need to give you a sense of worth, start by instigating the following cure to help you to know what you are looking for.

Place the Bagua over the plan of your home, and find where in your room or house the area Core is located. Incidentally, if you live in a house or a flat and have access to more than one room, then use the Bagua map over each room in turn, and bring in similar cures to each part of the room that corresponds to Core.

For direction as to what it is in a partner or relationship you are looking for, place a gold or silver ring, a piece of gold-leaf paper or a silver candlestick in the Core area. Gold and silver are both highly auspicious in Feng Shui, not only to promote prosperity, but also to vitalize integrity and determination in your life.

2 Do I have a problem attracting someone?

If this is your major concern, you may feel that you're never going to find a partner and consequently never feel attractive yourself. To allow yourself to attract and magnetize, use the following placement as a valuable source of self-empowerment. Place the Bagua over the plan of your home and find where the area Fire is located. To give you more confidence and belief in yourself, and to empower yourself with magnetic charm, place either a prism, if you can get one, or a red-glass bowl or wine goblet in the Fire area of your home. Light some incense every evening in this area.

3 Do I have a problem maintaining a relationship?

Whatever the difficulties, to become more consistent

and aware of your relationships use the following cure in the area of your home in which Heaven is located. Place three or four pine cones in a wooden bowl in this part of your house, or even a small ceramic bowl of pine nuts – you can buy these from delicatessens and supermarkets these days. A bonsai pine tree adds more of an aesthetic touch to this placement, if you can find one. Mountain pines were often depicted in ancient Taoist art, and symbolized longevity and wisdom. They are grounding and bring self-awareness.

4 Do I always go for the wrong types?

The chemistry between two people is mysterious and irrational. But some of us frequently attract or fall in love with the wrong person. If this is a problem for you, use the following cure in the Heaven area of your home to improve your perspective and help you connect to the right types. Either hang a small piece of the crystal Sodalite in the Heaven area of the room or, if you can't get hold of a piece, hang a mirror sconce on a wall so that it reflects both the source of natural light during the day and the lamp or candlelight itself.

5 Why did I split up with my partner?

This can be a torturous and regretful space to be in. If you feel as if you have no courage left and that there must be something wrong with you, or that your partner treated you badly, use the following cure in the Wind area of your home to begin to be at peace with yourself so that you can enjoy happiness again. Hang a Rose Quartz crystal from your window, or place it where the natural light will beam its self-loving qualities out to you.

6 Why can't I stop thinking about X?

To enable you to forget someone, or to readjust your perception of who they are and why you may be hurting or pining for them, use the following cure in the Lake area of your home. Take two candles – one white, one black – and stand them together in front of a window pane or a mirror. A window is better because at night when you light the black candle, the reflection in the glass is more powerful than in a mirror. It draws the uncomfortable feelings away, but illuminates and reflects the energies associated with the white candle. Light both together. Once the black candle dies away, you will see yourself and your desire with clarity.

In the next chapter you can begin to focus on even more personal ways of enjoying your relationships and improving them in the long term, whether single or not. But remember, don't expect instantaneous results. Feng Shui is a process that works out there in your environment and within you. It may work with the speed of lightning if you *sincerely trust* in what you are doing. If you find things aren't changing as quickly as you expect, don't try filling your environment with too many cures at once. Go back to the beginning and open only one pathway at a time. And – most important – enjoy what you are doing!

Chapter Seven

Your Lovestyle Location

What does 'love' actually mean to you? In contemporary Western society a belief has evolved that when you grow up, you fall in love and get married to the person with whom you fall in love. That magical moment of desire, then of ecstasy and physical bliss, of mystery and magic and romance, is meant to be something that marriage can contain.

The problem we face today is trying to understand that romantic and physical love is not necessarily the answer to long-term happiness. Marriage or a long-term partnership doesn't automatically have to include the romantic option. We cannot expect another human being to carry all that baggage for us, nor can we be expected to carry it for them. We seek romance, we seek friendship, we seek transformation of pain and suffering, we seek to merge with something other than ourselves. Because religion seems to have let us down, we think we can find divine and spiritual love and a meaning in life through someone else.

To expect so much from a partner can cause an overload and set up an imbalance both within yourself and within the subject of your choice. There's nothing wrong with romance and eroticism – they are wonderful, magical things – but we have to learn that such moments don't last for ever. They may evolve into different kinds of love, but because we are so infatuated with being 'in love' we only ever look for this kind of fulfilment in our lives.

This may sound horribly negative, especially if you're in the throes of a passionate love affair, or you feel you have merged with your lover and will never look back. True, there are a few 'happy ever after' couples, but it is naive to assume that everyone will find eternal romance with one partner. Often romantic love gets lost among the nappies and the routine of living, which is when many people troop off to find that passion again in someone else's eyes.

Early Chinese magicians and Feng Shui masters wisely knew that harmony of spirit and body was essential. They worked with their sexuality and did not necessarily marry for 'love'. As in many other cultures, marriage or monogamy in ancient China was about money, harmony and raising children. Friendship became the core of long-term relationships, and often erotic and romantic love played very little part in them. Meaning in life was sought through a spiritual path, and divine love was not an expectation of a human relationship.

Love wears many masks, and the only one we can be sure about is the one we are experiencing at this moment. The purest love of all is unconditional love; but how often have you met anyone who can live up to that? And can you?

Here are the lovestyles. First of all, ask yourself the question: What does love mean to me now? Is it . . .

Romance
'Falling in love'

Mystery
Affairs/Excitement/Dangerous games
Communication
Nurturing another person
Being nurtured
Companionship/Friendship
Purely physical
Eroticism
Passion
Emotional entanglement
Being possessed
Possessing
Pain and suffering
Letting go – ecstasy and agony
Power
Destruction
Freedom
Divine/otherworldly/universal

Some of these may sound like heavy duty words. But if you get in touch with your feelings and needs, whether in a current relationship or reflecting on a past or recent one, you may be surprised at what love means to you. If you have a lover, ask them if they can connect to any of these words, too.

Can you see yourself in the Bagua lovestyle mirror in Figure 18? Once you have decided which of the Bagua energies is how you are feeling right now about love – not yesterday, not tomorrow, not how you think you should feel, but right *now* – then you can start to channel harmony into this area of your home and your heart.

Figure 18: Bagua lovestyle mirror.

How to create harmony in the Bagua mirror

Place the Bagua over the plan of your room, flat or house. By referring to the lovestyle Bagua you can see which area of your home relates to the way you feel. This is the location of your home in which to place cures and make changes that can bring harmony to the way you personally love.

First use the Bagua grid over your whole house or home as a guide to the main location of the Bagua energy. You can use the Bagua over specific areas too, like a special room, the garden, the hallway, the front entrance, the bedroom, the place you work, even your desk. Simply place the Bagua over a plan of this focal area and instigate cures in the same way. By placing cures in other areas that correspond to the main lovestyle location, you are working on many different levels of harmony at once.

For example, Emma was worried that her boyfriend was beginning to get cold feet, and suspected he might have met someone else. Although Steve didn't often spend the night at her house, when he did they always seemed to have arguments even before they got into bed. She decided to place a cure in the Thunder areas of her home, believing that someone else might be involved with Steve, or some-one was interfering with his feelings.

Figure 19 shows you how the Bagua pattern lay over Emma's house. Figure 20 demonstrates how Emma used the Bagua again in the bedroom to see where Thunder was sited in her room.

When you use the Bagua for a room, line up the door-way (the main doorway if there are two doors) with the base

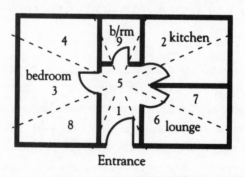

Figure 19: Emma's flat.

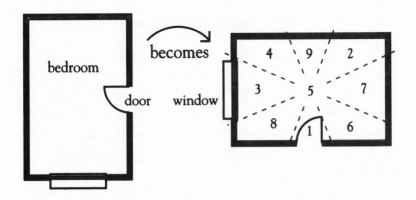

Figure 20: Emma's bedroom, with the Bagua realigned on the doorway.

of the Bagua where Water begins. If your room is oddly shaped or has projections or indentations, use the simple method shown in Figure 6, page 26, to determine the centre of the room and line up the centre of the Bagua to this instead, and extend it to cover the whole room.

In this example, Thunder fell across the area under Emma's window where there was a chair and a pile of books. The only way to reach the window was by standing on the wobbly old chair. Emma removed the chair and the books, and hung some wind chimes from the window frame. Within a couple of weeks Steve became more relaxed at her house. He even became less aggressive in the bedroom and at one point admitted that he had felt as if someone had always been 'sitting in judgement' on him when he was in her room. He'd felt threatened by the previous men in her life she had sometimes mentioned. The Thunder was referring to the intrusion of her own past, rather than anyone in Steve's life.

Cures and enhancements

This section explains how to use the cures and enhancements for your birth element in your current lovestyle location. Don't forget, your lovestyle can change and evolve, just as you do. Once you have worked with the area of your home which is the reflection of your lovestyle now, you may find in six months' time that you choose another lovestyle and need to make changes in another part of your home.

Don't use all the cures at once! Pick out one colour, one object, one design and enjoy them, rather than trying to throw everything into the lovestyle location at once.

If you're Fire

Fire does well when Wood cures are incorporated into your lovestyle location. Wood nourishes Fire and makes it feel comfortable, stoked up, alight, and sometimes flaming with passion! However, never overdo these cures. If you start filling your lovestyle location with wooden furniture and plants, green walls and green carpets and a library's worth of books, you'll overload the element. Wood will start to take over and you'll be back to square one with an energy that won't or can't move or vitalize for you.

You respond to colours that are red, hot, shiny and bold, but your lovestyle location needs the balance and incorporation of Wood or Earth colours to harmonize the excessive energy of your Fire personality. You may love passionately and ardently, but you need to surround yourself with natural colours to ground your sense of powerful love. Choose one of the Wood colours in your lovestyle location – greens, country tones associated with herbs – sage, rosemary, thyme, cool peppermints; forest greens and soft pinky hues of the sky in the morning. Earth colours are twilight blues and pistachio; gentle tones evocative of spring meadows, summer softness when the corn is high, and the mellow ochres and olive greens of the changing leaves in autumn. Earth colours can be as dark as coal, or as baked as terracotta. But avoid sickly yellows! You may feel subdued and depressed in such surroundings. Try to ensure you can see trees or gardens from the lovestyle location; if you can't, hang a photo or picture of a landscape beside the window.

Bring a wooden sculpture or bits of old gnarled wood found on the beach into your lovestyle location. If you're not keen on actual wood, then compromise with one majestic sculptural plant such as a mother-in-law's tongue or a spreading ficus. Wood cures can help you to kick-start any dying passion in your sex life.

Illustrations for your walls can be either bold and direct paintings or photography and line drawings with purer definition. These add the qualities of Wood and Earth, and blend both elements at once. The softer hues of watercolours are more likely to bring harmony into your lovestyle location, whereas garish colour might make your passion turn inward against yourself.

Books are a good source of Wood energy. Although collecting a library is not a particularly fiery pursuit (and you're unlikely to keep the place in order), there are ways of adding books – such as a mural of false books – to this area without resorting to the antiquarian bookshop.

If the lovestyle location happens to be in a bathroom, the Wood and Earth cures come into their own, with shells, stones and useful items made from natural products such as loofahs and sponges. If it's in the kitchen, old glass jars filled with exotic spices, like cinnamon sticks and coriander seeds, will do the same work. Anything that comes from the ground can be lined up on a kitchen shelf. Bring in leafy plants such as ivies and climbers that spread and scramble rather than trail (but not spider plants, which will depress a Fire person as soon as they enter the room). Monolithic cacti and giant rubber plants are not recommended for Fire. Too much competition!

Finally, a single Metal cure can be integrated into your lovestyle location to ensure successful loving. Add a touch of gold paint, or paint gold stars on a door or wall. Gold is better than silver for Fire. Gilded furniture or picture frames are more subtle enhancements. If the lovestyle location of your bedroom is situated right over the bed, gold jewellery or mock-gold costume baubles hung from your bedposts can do wonders to liven up the inspirational side of your sex life.

If you're Earth

You are usually in touch with your surroundings, even if you don't take a special interest in beauty. Earth responds extremely well to the Fire and Metal cures in the lovestyle location, but you can feel muddy if you're surrounded by too much Water and distinctly static with too much Wood! Too many plants and natural objects in your environment play havoc with your senses. Because you need to express your close connection to the natural world, Wood is better channelled through working with plants or animals; gardening, growing vegetables, helping reclaim woods and hedges, or just getting out into the countryside if you live in a town.

In the lovestyle location of your home use Fire and

Metal cures. Too much Wood can drain your energy, so if this part of your home is filled with wooden furniture or plants, try to relocate as many of these items as possible. Bring Fire cures such as white candles, gilt-edged mirrors and subdued lighting into the lovestyle location. There is so much choice in lighting these days; what about those art nouveau swan-necked wall lights or art deco styles made of Bakelite and onyx? These kinds of lighting add vitality without taking over the senses. Alternatively, if your lovestyle location is in the kitchen, use cast-iron or stainless steel cooking pots and pans. Invest in a stainless steel work-surface if you feel rich. Designs in gold leaf or gold powder painted on ancient bits of tatty furniture are excellent Metal cures for the lovestyle location. Some scrap metal placed aesthetically in the corresponding area of your garden, backyard or even the bathroom can be an extraordinarily powerful evocation of Metal for harmonizing your way of loving!

Choose one vibrant colour and a more luminous airy colour to complement your deeply pantheistic spirit. Your aesthetic skills are probably highly evolved so make use of colour co-ordination. Choose fabric that suggests a tone, wallpaper that picks up on a theme – different elements engaged in mutual passion. Try toning your walls with colourwashes, tints and dramatically different coloured woodwork. Use soft sheen colours or eggshell paint rather than gloss. Fiery colours like Indian reds, brilliant whites and smoking-jacket red, crimsons and tangerine orange could add a zest to your sensual sexuality. Use one Water colour for sexual expressiveness and for physical motivation – dark mystical violet, viridian, Prussian blue or even black. If the bedroom is a focus of your lovestyle location use a fabric cure such as cushions or curtains that are made from faded damask, or old French tapestry. A Metal cure in your bedroom such as an iron bedstead brings you instant affirmation of your physical needs.

If you're Metal

Although silver and gold are the definitive expressions of Metal and are often emphasized in Eastern cultures because of the value that is placed on importing them into your home, remember that by surrounding yourself with too much of your own element, you may bring about exaggeration of Metal in your love life. This could make you incredibly wealthy, but it won't make you particularly happy. Greed is not the same as hunger. Contentment and tranquillity are about knowing when to stop; so, too, is happiness.

To harmonize your lovestyle location use Water and Earth cures. Wood is also useful but you've probably got enough furniture and books to make up the Wood element in the lovestyle location anyway. Earth and Water cures will bring a sense of sharing and communication into your lovestyle. Shells picked up on a beach, smooth pebbles, weathered stones or fragments of glass polished by the waves are easily incorporated. Flint stones are especially energizing for Metal, though they may be difficult to find if you don't live in the right area of the country. Any ancient pieces of rock you pick up on country walks or even city ones will do. Add a pure pink shell from the beach. If you don't have access to the seaside or the country, choose an *unpolished* piece of amber and place it on the window ledge of your lovestyle location.

Paintings of the sea, photos of lakes, perhaps a simple Japanese landscape drawing or print would be useful to vitalize your lovestyle location. Water-colours can be depressing for you, but place a bowl full of coloured blue and black marbles on the highest surface in your room. You may not be able to see the Water hues, yet they will be working for you. You would probably find that adding one of Earth's warm terracottas, yellow ochres, rich umbers or burnt siennas to your colour scheme in the lovestyle location, especially if this corresponds to your kitchen or bathroom, would help point you towards a better understanding of how you need to relate to others.

A picture framed in black or ebonized wood will add a magical touch of Water's elusiveness to your location. Black and dark blues could also be captured and hinted at in fabrics, particularly bed covers, blinds, curtains and cushions. Try to avoid wrought iron and metal furniture – although it may appeal, it can stimulate your energy like a highly charged magnet and produce extremes of feeling, confusing your sense of commitment and integrity.

If you're Water

Even though Wood and Metal are the best cures for Water, Water needs to be grounded first. So Earth cures must also be included in the lovestyle location. To vitalize your love, incorporate a crystal or a rock that has originated from river-beds or the sea such as Coral or Malachite. A fossil or even several pebbles and stones in a glass jar or stone pot are also auspicious cures. Wood is an animating cure to include in your location. Best of all for harmony, either find a carving of a bird – the freedom that birds symbolize is important here – or a simply carved piece of furniture or wooden jewellery. Music is a cure that reduces your anxiety and your over-sensitivity to others. This is perhaps one of the best reasons for using wind chimes in your lovestyle location. However, there is now a wide and varied choice of wind chimes, so make sure you choose the ones which have the right harmonies to your ear, rather than the most fashionable. If you haven't any musical instruments in your home, get hold of a recorder, a flute, a cello, a piano – whatever you can afford – and play music in your lovestyle location. If this happens to be the bathroom or loo, then just sing! Music is flowing, and can enhance your love life because it is expressing your Water nature, rather than sucking it in.

Fire cures include white candles and sandalwood incense. Fabrics can be rich and vividly coloured. If your lovestyle location is in the bedroom, either sleep in a four-poster bed or, if that is impossible, try to find a painting or a print of a wild mountainous landscape and hang it above your bed. If your lovestyle location is in the kitchen, make sure you include a good selection of spices and dramatic lighting above your cooking area.

Do bring a Metal cure into this location if you can, as it may help to focus your vision of love. If you are fond of silver be sure you use it quietly, for silver may make Water types more sensitive than they already are! Obviously not many of us can afford the luxury of real gold objets d'art, or even gold bangles, but as long as you include some pretend gold in your interior design, in the form of colour, brass and copper pots and pans, then Metal doesn't have to be heavily invasive in your home.

Include a vibrant shade such as fuchsia or turquoise in your colour scheme. Take, for example, red as a theme for your bedroom or paint everything white and add colours in dramatic contrast to add that Fire sparkle, then the energy will begin to vitalize your own inner beauty.

If you're Wood

Fire is a magical and creative element for Wood, so, if you can, add a candelabrum, chandelier or lighting in bright colours. If your lovestyle location is in the kitchen, make sure you have a powerful light source when cooking or entertaining. Another excellent Fire cure is to hang a string of dried chilli peppers in your kitchen beside the back door. This can help keep the Fire burning through any love affair! It may have a spirited effect on your communication with long-term partners. If you haven't got an open fireplace, hang paintings or photos that have some element of fire about them – anything from a mellow scene of autumnal bonfires to a cosmic explosion of stars. If the lovestyle location is in your bathroom, light candles to bathe by or listen to Fire music – whether it's 'Smoke Gets In Your Eyes' or 'London's Burning'! Either way you are bringing both cures into your lovestyle location in one expression of energy. If you're working with your bedroom, try to find an old piece of stained glass and lean it in the window to catch the early morning or evening sun.

Wood also needs a simple Water cure in the lovestyle location. This can be an aquarium, a fish tank or just an elegant bath, basin or shower. If you're lucky enough to have one, enjoy the pond in the garden; if you're in a flat, bedsit or room, draw a picture of your ideal pond or find old prints of dragonflies and frogs. Terracotta pots in the kitchen or a group of pebbles outside your front door are simple ways to bring grounding Earth energy into your lovestyle location.

Avoid Metal in your lovestyle location as it is highly destructive for Wood, and can lead you into believing there is no value in individual or intimate relationships. However, wear Metal in the form of jewellery to add status to your already sophisticated lifestyle. Water cure colours such as deep royal blues and blue-blacks like ink can do much to put you in touch with your feelings. Again choose one or two Earth colours such as ochres, sludge browns and coffee or tea shades to bring balance and a more physical and sensual expression to your love life.

Chapter Eight

How to Create a Dynamic Loving Relationship

Here is a quick and easy guide to the cures you need for a dynamic loving relationship. If you have a happy or fairly harmonious relationship already, then you can use these remedies for enhancement as well.

The Sticks and Stones Test

The Sticks and Stones Test is a great way for checking out what state your current relationship is in and also, perhaps more importantly, whether you want to make changes to your relationship or not. The problem is that once we've got past the romantic dinner and thinking of sex stage, things start to move along in a linear fashion, rather than flow through the spirals of love and romance. In the beginning of a relationship there are ups and downs, conflicts and passions, envy and hate, feelings and denials – all usually played out in each other's arms. But the big quest to form a partnership often ends up with the ball of romance and passion bobbing on a flat empty sea where no one wants to play. For some people this is fine. We don't especially need the conflicts, dramas, aches and pains of love. But for many of us, just when we think everything is wonderful we find the relationship has lost its spice, there is no conflict, no risk, and we do battle with our partner just for the sake of it.

First is a list of points associated with what I call the Sticks relationship.

Sticks Relationship

1 *No secrets* – you keep nothing of yourself for yourself.

2 *Social cloning* – you both join the same social groups, have identical friends, always go round in a twosome. (Some couples even dress alike.)

3 *Specific roles* – for example, she always plays the mother, housekeeper, cook, secretary, Madonna, the hurt one, the cross one; he always plays father, breadwinner, boss, Rudolph Valentino (if you're lucky), the alcoholic, the workaholic.

4 *Nil objectives* – or at the most, aiming to remain safe and secure in the nest.

5 *Self-deceit* – believing your current existence is going to last for ever, unchanging.

6 *Romance is dead* – no passion, anger or emotion is shown.

7 *Static lifestyle* – routines, both daily and sexual, are established.

8 *Restricted communication.*

9 *Power struggle* – controller versus the one who doesn't want to be controlled.

10 *Won't take risks.*

11 *Dependent on each other* – i.e., one acts out parent role, the other child role. Overtly nurturing relationship.

12 *Inseparable or always wishing for more.*

If you recognize yourself in this list and feel inclined to liven things up, look at the list below of signs that may be missing in your relationship. These are to be found in what I call the Stones relationship. Again, no relationship is probably this extreme, but these are factors that can be incorporated into a stale Sticks relationship to help it work and/or evolve.

If you feel that any of these Stones qualities are missing from your relationship, turn to the detailed section which follows and look up which area of the Bagua to enhance. Place your Bagua over the plan of your house, flat or room and see where in your home this particular Bagua energy flows so that you know where to incorporate the cures.

Stones Relationship

1 *Secrets* – you keep something of yourself to yourself.

2 *Social interaction and variety* – you share the same friends but also have your own chums.

3 *Changing roles* – she can be the boss and he can be the housewife; he can have feelings and she can have her space.

4 *Positive objectives* – you both want the relationship to evolve, to grow, to change, to stay erotic.

5 *Trust* – acceptance of the space and boundary of your partner; willingness to let go; awareness that relationships change.

6 *Eros is alive and kicking* – passion, anger and pain are

often essential to maintain a dynamic and living relationship.

7 *Dynamic lifestyle* – this doesn't mean non-stop sex or jet-setting round the world; it means moving, flowing, getting on with your life; being active and creative within the relationship.

8 *Good communication* – willingness to listen, not to be judgemental, to allow others their perception of the world.

9 *Active, changing* – letting your partner be who they are; your partner letting you be you.

10 *Risky* – giving you personal freedom to express your feelings, your needs, yourself.

11 *Independence.*

12 *Acceptance, not wishing for more.*

The missing qualities

In each case, place the appropriate cures in the corresponding parts of your house or room. Remember, you don't have to use all the cures at once.

1 If you have *missing secrets*, the Bagua area that may need enhancement is Earth.

Use either silver fabrics or creamy white paintwork; soft, muted colours such as ointment pink and buttermilk; wrought iron candle sconces or wrought iron or metal furniture. If your Earth area is in the bedroom, you can hang fake or real gold jewellery from the bedposts; if it's in the kitchen, hang loads of stainless steel pots and pans, but make sure you've got some metal utensils standing upright in jars to balance the 'falling' metal energy with 'growing' metal! Plants with strong vertical lines – pencil thin bamboos or fast-growing lilies (preferably white) – can be a striking feature in the kitchen and bring a sense of 'keeping something to oneself' to the relationship. If Earth is in the bathroom or loo, paint or stencil some silver stars on the walls of your bathroom, or add a magical touch of gold-leaf edging around the loo, so you don't end up losing all your secrets down the pan.

2 If you have *missing social interaction*, the Bagua area that may need enhancement is Thunder.

If your relationship revolves around 'our' friends and you seem to have few you can call your own, then you may need to bring a tank of goldfish into the Thunder area. Next time you're near a beach, pick up shells or even dried seaweed. Make a shell 'picture' or simply pile a load of shells into a jar and stand them on the windowsill of your Thunder area. If Thunder happens to coincide with your loo or bathroom, hang seaweed around your bathroom mirror, but make sure you don't have any plants standing on top of the cistern. Placing an unusual wooden sculpture or a bronze statue in your Thunder area is a cure to give you a sense of being able to choose who you like and who you want to be with, rather than always relying on your partner for company. Wind chimes will allow beneficial energy to circulate, and prevent unwelcome energy from becoming stagnant. By hanging a mirror on a wall to reflect the wind chimes you can incorporate a dash of carefree exuberance in your Thunder area. Dinner parties will never be the same again if you remember to place a yellow candle as a centrepiece surrounded by paper dragons or charms. These charms were often used as talismans to attract helpful friends into your life. Figure 21 is a talisman you can copy on to as many pieces

Figure 21: Shou, a talisman for long life and happiness with many friends.

of paper as you have friends for dinner. Roll them up and place them around the candle until dinner is finished. Give one to each guest on their departure.

3 If you have *missing role changing*, the Bagua area that may need enhancement is Heaven.

When we get stuck into being a housewife or a bread-winner, there seems no way out apart from leaving home. Yet by shifting your perspective of who you are and who your partner is, you will find you don't actually have to buy a new wardrobe or go to drama school to learn how to act out a part. Role changing is about saying, 'Look, here I am, *me*, not just a cook, not just a mother. I can be anything I want to be but that doesn't mean I'm going to turn into a werewolf overnight!' This is about not putting your partner into a category and not letting yourself be put into a category either. We all have to be cooks, nurses, wives, husbands, secretaries, bosses, etc., but we mustn't give up our true identity in the process. In a close partnership it's easy to lose track of who you really are.

The Bagua area of Heaven in your house is the place where you can enhance your own sense of identity, and also the way you view your partner and vice versa. By incorporating some of the following cures you can begin to activate that process of *me*-ness. A single white candle or a large White Quartz crystal can vitalize the Heaven location. To enable you both to be more aware of each other, you should choose vibrant colours. Wherever Heaven is in your home, use rich reds and bold primaries to keep you mentally alert and active. Copy the talisman in Figure 17, page 72, and either paint or draw it on the door that leads out of your Heaven area to encourage the energy to circulate.

If Heaven happens to be in the kitchen, ensure that your cooker is facing good natural light. Interior lighting can also be bold and expressive, or warm and glowing at night to emphasize the atmosphere you feel truly reflects you.

4 If you have *missing positive objectives*, the Bagua area that may need enhancement in your home is Earth.

If your relationship is like a still pond, you may feel bored with sex, bored with the kids, lethargic and generally bored with life. You may have known each other six months or six years, it doesn't matter how long before the static quality starts to sink in. What you have to remember is that it's easy to fall into an armchair and ignore what is going on . . . zzz!

If an evolving and enriching relationship appeals to you and you want to learn more about yourself and your partner, enhancing the Earth area of your home may enable you at least to begin to desire change and variety in your love life. First, you should go out and find a piece of Lapis Lazuli or Azurite. Place the piece of stone in a window of your Earth location or at least on a table near good daylight sources. If you can't get hold of either of these stones, use pebbles and shells or fill terracotta pots with scented geraniums. Evocative scents are as transformative and as sensual as the vibrations of crystals. Choose an erotic colour to incorporate into your decoration. Either deep wine silk sheets if it's a bedroom location, or midnight blue or raspberry pink cushions and curtains if it's the living room. In the kitchen, make sure you always have a plate of figs, passion fruit, apricots or peaches on the table. Quails' eggs were an erotic delicacy for the ancient Chinese but, if you're not fond of raw eggs, paint a wooden egg with gold leaf and hang it from a beam or corner of your Earth room to vitalize erotic feelings.

Finally, use fake animal furs, paintings of tigers and wild animals or even tiger's eye gemstones in your Earth area as cures for bringing back the drama to flagging desire.

5 If you have *missing trust*, the area of the Bagua that may need enhancement in your home is Wind.

If you cannot feel that you trust your partner, how can you trust yourself? One of the most important cures for jealousy and mistrust is to place a piece of yellow Peridot (a semi-precious stone) in the Wind area of your home. Its vibrant chartreuse colour needs to be recharged with the sun's rays, so make sure it is near a natural source of light. If you are unable to find this stone, use yellow marbles or pieces of glass in a glass bowl. Another way to bring missing trust back into your relationship is to place a bowl of pine cones or pine nuts near the window. Alternatively, get out into the countryside or down by the sea and find flotsam and jetsam or storm-damaged branches; paint walls and use fabrics in muted olive greens, duck-egg blues and ochre yellows. Wind chimes are invaluable because they redirect difficult energy and enhance the harmony of good vibrations. Another wonderfully powerful way to bring trust into your heart is by hanging glass crystals or beads from a table lamp – a bit like a glass chandelier. These can be any colour, but avoid too many white or clear ones – and the more yellow and green you use the better!

6 If you have *missing Eros*, the area of the Bagua that may need enhancement in your home is Lake.

This is one thing that many of us quickly miss when it is lacking in our relationship. Unfortunately sexual passion often begins to wane as the years clock on by. The big illusion is assuming romance is part of the package of marriage or long-term partnerships. The truth is that it is not always the case. Sexual pleasure and physical desire are the things which usually draw us together, and sometimes the things that tear us apart.

Your sex life is incredibly important, so when you place the Bagua over your plan and find where Lake is in your house, it is worth creating a magic corner here and placing some of the cures here so that you can keep this powerful area of your home as a special and creative place.

Sensuality and sexuality are very different. To create both within a dull relationship, or one that may be in danger of losing its sparkle, bring incense, flowers, gemstones, crystals and stunning colours into this part of your house to inspire Eros back. The best incense for stirring sexual passion is Patchouli or opium (not the drug, but it is made from the same poppy). The woody-scented ones such as Sandalwood also work well. The ancient Chinese were avid incense burners, particularly when they were trying to achieve immortality through their sexual performances. If you find that burning incense fills your lungs with smoke rather than clears the air and energizes the vital essences, dab perfume on your pillows, your sheets and your body if the Lake area of the Bagua happens to be in the bedroom. If it isn't here, find the Lake area within your bedroom and use scents or perfumed candles. If Lake is located in the bathroom, always bathe in exotic oils or spicy sensual foam. Aromatherapy oils are perfect for dribbling into the bath or shower.

The Chinese used fruit and flowers as cures and sexual enhancers. The obvious ones are figs, pomegranates and peaches. Place a bowl of dried cloves and pomegranate seeds in the Lake area. In the summer stand a jug of wild poppies on the window ledge to drop their petals in your Lake area. When the seed heads are dry, empty the seeds into the bowl with the cloves and pomegranates. Finding poppies out of season is obviously impossible, so in winter, paint poppies on to a cupboard or wall, or hang up a picture of wild poppies. If you have any plates that are painted or decorated with flowers such as peonies, poppies, lilies or magnolia, make sure you always eat off them if your Lake area is in the kitchen. The sexual qualities of these flowers were believed to be transmitted to the food on your plate and then absorbed by eating the food – a quick way to feed your lover with erotic energy! Gourds are wonderfully evocative of the union of

Heaven and Earth, or the sexual combination of male and female. Gourds in a bowl on the window ledge can bring good sexual energy into your Lake area.

If you have a peach or plum tree nearby, in spring or summer carefully cut a few branches of the blossom and bring it into your Lake area. Plum blossom is particularly auspicious for creative sexual energy. In the winter, plant a bowl of richly scented hyacinths as a growing energy in your Lake area. Build up a mound of pebbles or beautiful stones beside the doorway or the entrance to the Lake area too.

Candles are wonderful sexual enhancers. The choice is incredible now, so indulge yourself in the luxury of a gathering of candles, as many different shapes as possible as long as they are all red, orange, crimson and even black. Be outrageous and transform the Lake area of your home into a wilderness of candles (at least twenty!) and make love on the floor. It's as simple as that.

Bring some dramatic colour into your Lake area. Use black, cranberry, raspberry, cobalt blue, or deep red and turquoise together! Use deep red wine colours and midnight blues to bring a touch of bohemian aristocracy to the Lake area to arouse those erotic passions.

Finally, if you need more tender loving, more gentle and romantic passion, place a piece of Rose Quartz in the heart of the Lake area to activate love and harmony in your physical embraces.

7 If you have *missing dynamic lifestyle*, the area of your home that may be in need of enhancement is Fire.

A creative relationship is one where we make things happen, we actively bring about changes and are aware of our purpose in doing so. 'Dynamic' means a moving force or a pattern of growth and change. If you want yourself and your partner to get off the wheel of inertia, you need to apply your own personal dynamics. Routine is part of life whether we like it or not, and some of us thrive on knowing when we get up, when we go to bed, when we eat and when we make love. If you are happy with clocking on in all aspects of life, that's OK. If you're ready to abandon boring routines and bring more spontaneity and impulse into your love life, make a few changes in the Fire area of your home.

Use strong colours like red and gold together. Mirrors are essential in this area, especially if you can find ones with gilt frames or at least faux gold-leaf edges; if Fire happens to be in your sitting room and you've got a mantelpiece, find the biggest mirror you can and hang it over the fireplace. Silver is also a cure for getting relationships shifting. If you have anything made of silver, place it in the Fire area of your home and ensure it is reflected by a mirror. This doubles its energizing qualities. If your Fire area happens to be the kitchen or the loo, use stainless steel kitchen utensils stood in pots or stand a bowl of silver coins on top of the cistern. But make sure you keep the loo seat shut as you don't want to lose your energy down the drain. Find a White Quartz crystal and hang it in the window. The more imperfect the cut of the stone the better the light refracts, creating dimensions of light and rainbow colours to direct that dynamic energy back into your life.

8 If you have *missing communication*, enhance the areas of your home that relate to Mountain.

This is a big subject. Briefly, if you find your communication has broken down, that you never really talk like you used to do, or every time you open your mouth there's friction and bickering, make some changes in Mountain.

This energy really needs to flow, so bring in water cures. A glass bowl of coloured water filled with sea shells can enhance the deeper qualities of communication. Fish tanks and aquaria are common in Chinese homes and offices, and the essence of Water is easily energized by a shoal of shimmering tropical fish. However it's not always practical to have these wondrous creatures in your home. A single goldfish in a bowl is not to be recommended, first because the quality of life for that fish will be poor and second because this will reflect on your own communicative energy. If a tank of fish isn't possible for you, use images of fish and the beautiful creatures of the sea instead. If the Mountain area of your home is in the bathroom or loo, you can make use of shells, fish pictures, tiles with sea anemone or seaweed designs, and images of dolphins, whales and mermaids.

If Mountain happens to be in the kitchen, use Water colours such as inky blues and violets in your decor. Seascapes and paintings of waterfalls, rivers, beaches, cliffs and foaming surf are all excellent Water enhancers because they stimulate the flow of energy. If you are lucky enough to live near the sea or a large expanse of water that is flowing, attempt to place your comfortable sofa, kitchen chairs or bed to face the view. Never turn your back on Water: it's like standing below the level of high tide and expecting it never to turn and come back in! If it's not practical to rearrange your furniture or your view of Water, place a piece of Amber in your window to draw in any difficult external energy. Not really a crystal, Amber is pine tree sap that has been petrified millions of years ago, and often holds within it beautiful insects and tiny creatures. Its power is incomparable. After placing Amber on a window ledge for some time, you may find it becomes cloudy. This means it's working. To prevent the Amber from sending back the difficult energy it has absorbed, clean it carefully once in a while to discharge this energy in Water.

Finally, if Mountain happens to be in your hallway, hang a line of flying ducks up the wall to create good flowing energy. In fact any bird images can be great communication enhancers.

9 If you have *missing active change*, the areas of your home which may be in need of cures are Fire and Heaven. Both of these areas are important for creating harmony so place a cure in each if you can.

Truly altruistic love means that we do not possess or have rights over other people and their lives or feelings. This is a difficult vision of love to combine with monogamy, and for most of us ideal freedom within a relationship is hard to achieve. Asking too much from one relationship seems to be why marriage often doesn't quite fulfil its ideal; letting the other person be who they are, allowing them space and giving yourself space will, at least, go some way towards a more adult way of loving.

To activate change in your relationship, make subtle enhancements in the Fire and Heaven areas of your home. Wood cures are excellent for creating harmony and at the same time establishing a sense of freedom and space. Plants can be as exotic as you like and are possibly the easiest way to bring freedom into your Fire or Heaven areas. Another vitalizing cure is a piece of Tourmaline or Aquamarine. Tourmaline is one of the most beautiful of stones, and helps us combine the energizing quality of the universe with an enhanced sense of our own self-worth. Place a piece of Tourmaline near the entrance or doorway of your Fire and Heaven areas to activate this beautiful energy. Books are essential in one of these areas, as is some image or visual representation of a staircase or journey. Even a scene of wooden steps in a painting or a photo, or actual steps leading into or out of your Heaven area, can introduce energy that takes away control and power, and balances the give and take in a relationship. (Journeys take you somewhere, and so do stairs.) Wood in the form of paper is an easy incorporation – paper flowers, origami or paper sculptures are just as auspicious as carved oak. However, acorns are subtle enhancers and energize your own sense of who you are. Acorns grow into oak trees, just as we grow into ourselves.

10 If you have *missing risks*, the area of your home that may be in need of a cure is Water.

This doesn't mean being sneaky and having affairs; nor does it mean gambling with your money or your heart. Risk is about spontaneous thinking, about spontaneous loving. Risk is about taking a chance because you don't have time to plan or analyse or dissect to make decisions. It's the thrill of never knowing what is going to happen next – so bring risk back into your love life.

When you place the Bagua map over the plan of your home, you may find that the Water area is your hallway or around your front door. If it is, make sure that your stairs are well lit and that the door is uncluttered and free from badly fitting locks or keys. If you can't open or close the door smoothly, you won't allow the good energy to flow into or the difficult energy to flow out of your home. Bring vibrant colours to this area so that it grows with passion and desire.

Use fuchsia pink or raspberry red, lime green or buttercup yellow. Use a colour that talks to you as you walk through the door! Turquoise, gold and red together help to inspire spontaneous thinking. If you can, incorporate sconces on the wall. The reflected light from the candles will energize the location every time you walk in or out of the door. Make sure you don't have mirrors facing out into the garden, or you'll only bounce the energy back outside. It needs careful channelling if it is to be used positively. Place a piece of Carnelian or Bloodstone opposite your mirror, to bring pure wickedness and impulse back into your relationships.

If Water falls in any other part of the home you may be able to use a real fireplace. Burn wood rather than coal if you can, and throw some dried cloves, cinnamon sticks or incense on the fire to invoke the sparks of mystery. Hang dramatic paintings or prints of erotic Japanese or Chinese art above your bed if the Water area of your bedroom happens to correspond to your bed. If your bed is elsewhere, try to move it into the Water area of your bedroom – then you may find that spontaneity and excitement will turn up between the sheets as well. Wherever Water falls in your home, turn these areas into danger zones to activate your own passion for risks and challenges.

11 If you have *missing independence*, the area of the Bagua in need of enhancement may be Core.

Once a relationship has gone through the first romance and feeling of needing to be with that special other person night and day, some of us find our own identity and individualism returns pretty quickly, while others find it difficult to let go of their mutual dependence. This can result in, for example, the classic parent–child relationship where one acts out mum or dad and the other the child.

Independence means that you don't depend on someone else to feel OK. You don't need validation from outside yourself to be at one with yourself. This is about autonomy and self-esteem, about respect for self and respect for others. Maintaining a healthy sense of who you are so that you can function alone, knowing you can say no and retain your own needs and values, means you can be independent of someone and still love them for who they are.

The cures for missing independence can be brought into the Core area of your home. If you are feeling dependent on your partner for everything, place a single Diamond or a piece of Selenite or White Quartz crystal here. Make sure you put it on a white fabric – white velvet, even a piece of felt or silk will do – and on a table or surface which faces the sun. The light must energize the facets of the crystal, and the white surface won't soak up the energy that is needed for you. For more self-respect and a greater sense of autonomy within, use a gilt- or silver-framed mirror and place a single white candle in front of it. Light it when you are feeling vulnerable. A bag of old coins or a trail of silver necklaces hung from the window frame is a cure that can vitalize your own needs and values. If the Core area happens to be in your kitchen, cooking utensils standing in jars, copper-bottomed pots hanging on the walls or a simple metal sculpture can all enhance and energize your independence. If the Core area is in your bedroom, invest in a metal-framed four-poster so you can both sleep together – but know you can sleep alone too!

12 If you have *missing acceptance*, the area of your home that may be in need of a cure is Mountain.

Acceptance is about not trying to change others into something you think they should be. We all sometimes go into relationships with a vague and vain hope that we can redeem someone – which, in a way, shows our need to control and take over that person's identity to fit in with our own projections. When we fail, this either comes back to us with a vengeance or we retreat, leave and find another lover. What we have to learn is that you can't change anyone into being something they don't want to be. You have to accept them as they are.

If you find it difficult to accept your lover's differences, or that no one can live up to an ideal, you may have to place cures in the Mountain area of your home. Natural cures such as pebbles, gemstones and colours that have been generated from nature are easily incorporated into your Mountain areas. Use apricot, butterscotch, peach, camellia, coral, almond or clover on the walls or in your furnishings. Place a bowl of coloured water in the sunlight, or at least in a good source of natural light. The best stones for generating acceptance are Moonstones and Opals. Hang a string of Moonstones or Opals around a mirror in your Mountain area to vitalize your own emotional responsibility. If the Mountain area is in the loo or bathroom, ensure that you don't have plants on top of the cistern or trailing down from a shelf above. This is a sure way of directing acceptance down the drain! In the bathroom you can also use images of trees and landscapes, images of the sea or shells and colours that remind you of the wildness of the weather and the ocean. To energize acceptance we need both to ground our images and to allow them to flow. If the Mountain area turns out to be in the kitchen, make sure you keep the oven door shut at all times. Open oven doors allow our own energy to be drawn into the cooker and then burnt when it's turned up to 200 degrees. If you've got a microwave, keep well away from it when it's in use. The energy of a microwave can be difficult to deal with, but if you really have to have one, hang a string of garlic on the wall behind to diffuse this intrusive energy.

Chapter Nine

Enhancements and Cures for Sexual Harmony

If you have a lover or partner, this chapter gives you an exclusive journey down the pathway that leads to a creative and enriched sexual relationship. Now you know which element you are, and have probably looked up your partner's too, you can read the section for your combination of elemental lovers to harmonize and vitalize your physical relationship. Most of these cures are best incorporated in your bedroom. If you're single, take a trip down the road anyway. When you have opened the pathway for new love and created a magic space for someone new to enter your life, you'll be ready and waiting with a new wisdom.

This section is about having fun. Remember, your element sign refers to an archetype. We may not show all the qualities of our birth element, for, as in any astrology, there are many other factors involved.

Metal/Metal

'Beneath the lightning and the Moon . . . '

This kind of energy could be electrifying, and create an excessively sexual or physical relationship. The charge from two Metal types meeting can cause loads of spiralling energy centres in your home, particularly in bed. In some ways this may feel like a vortex of passion that sweeps you both off your feet. Each of you may be constantly battling to prove to the other who it is who is really on top. But, on the plus side, there is usually a highly magnetic and sexually charged atmosphere.

Ambitions for the relationship will involve creative and intellectual pursuits. However, both of you are capable of regeneration should the other one decide to jump out of the relationship when it feels too extreme. Loners together can make a powerful team, but will self-destruct if they can't live up to each other's need for autonomy. This is definitely an erotic relationship, but equally it could burn itself out quicker than it starts.

For sexual harmony

Make sure you keep the angles of the furniture in your bedroom soft and the lighting subdued. Energy has to move in spirals and curves to be effective; heavy edges and sharp angles make for difficulties. Hang floaty muslin curtains at open windows to ensure that the Ch'i circulates freely, to soothe some of that metallic friction. Incorporate a little Fire to keep your senses alert but don't overdo it. Use red candles and patchouli or jasmine incense to ensure you know where it is you are both going.

Bring Water into your life to make things flow. Have a bed which moves easily so you can keep changing your view of the ceiling or the walls, and a bubbling aquarium if you have the inclination and the space. If not, put on a tape of watery music – an erotic stream or a gurgling spring – to make love to. Plug into each other's torrid and dedicated drive to achieve sexual mastery and hang mirrors where you can see yourself perform. However, avoid sleeping directly below or in front of a mirror as this can bring difficult energy into your sleeping patterns. Use a red duvet cover, or silk sheets to remind you that sensuality is an art. If you find there's a short circuit in the bed, turn it to face west and enjoy the sunset.

To harmonize your relationship on an emotional level, ensure that you bring Earth into your home in the guise of serene and elegant surroundings. Sensuality is a must; massage and aromatherapy oils or baths in spicy scents can do wonders for your sense of touch. Use calming colours such as peach, coral or camellia on the walls to inspire the genuine affection and awareness that a Metal partnership can cultivate.

Metal/Fire

'Two extremes of passion . . . burst smilingly.'

This can be a highly volatile relationship as the energy patterns between you will be dissimilar. In Feng Shui, Fire is an empowering adversary for Metal. The burning quality of Fire's desire and passion can leave Metal feeling melancholic and single-minded. If there is a strong magnetic chemistry to this relationship, it can work if both elements learn to give each other space to clarify their intense passions. If your sexual paths cross and what erupts is molten lava, this relationship can still survive if you both agree to drive down separate roads in other facets of your life.

Metal is single-minded and Fire is demanding; Metal is erotic and powerful, Fire is dynamic and daring. All these words convey two determined people each with a highly developed sense of self. This can make for two egos that pull each other apart in the battle for domination. Handled with care, it may be an exciting and dramatic relationship, but this kind of intensity can't survive for long without the threat of wiping itself out. For Fire the issues are self and self alone. Fire is strongly egotistic and wants everything *now*, while Metal seeks to dominate the world and teach it to sing. Metal can become a dictator or a saint.

For sexual harmony

Earth cures are needed in high doses! Try dabbing and spraying perfumes and incense over the sheets so that you both remember the natural sensuality of life. You are both individualists and passionate about it, so watch out that expressions of love don't turn into contests or heated debates across the pillows.

Keep a collection of comedy videos or blue movies for late night viewing. Humour is an essential element to incorporate into your volatile relationship. Make sex fun, laugh about your bodies and get tactile. Remember to communicate before you get down to the nitty-gritty. Keep a bowl of luscious fruit – peaches, apricots, mangoes and melons – near your bed. One of the most energizing cures for Metal/Fire is to place a piece of Pink Tourmaline near where you both sleep to activate awareness of love for others as well as for self. If you can't find this stone, use Rose Quartz.

If you have roamed beyond a purely physical relationship, bring Earth into your home via colour (yellows, ochres, russets) and nature. Choose plants with strong sculptural qualities; objets d'art with gentle curves; fossils, shells, paintings of form and places, rather than abstractions or drama. Water elements should be added with care and you might use the idea of flow in your environment rather than Water itself – flowing curtains, duvet covers that portray the image of water or the sea. In your bathroom hang pictures of waves and even sea creatures. But avoid still water, as this can make you depressed and turn your energy inward on itself until an already overloaded circuit shorts out.

Metal/Wood

'I never apologize.'

Metal destroys Wood in the cycle of elements and although passion can be aroused in the naturally laid-back and charming Wood personality it can also be engulfed by the highly volatile potency of Metal. With such opposite values in life – Metal requiring autonomy and ambition on their agenda and Wood with humanitarianism and freedom on theirs – this may be a relationship of beginnings and endings, of ambivalence and of distance. Physically, however, it could be highly creative if each begins to accept the other's viewpoint and melts towards a middle ground.

Unfortunately Metal people need to assert themselves and Wood prefers to avoid anyone who thinks they can. But it takes two to tango and this kind of dance, even in the short term, often turns into a flamenco display of outright anger from Metal and aloof complacency from Wood. Any polarity of elements can create enormous friction, and the energy surrounding a Metal/Wood connection can be disturbed by Metal's hunger for erotic mobility and Wood's need for detached and airy love-making. Metal may prefer the silence and intensity of secret sex, but Wood might well get a kick out of socializing with as many friends and exes as possible and reminiscing about past lovers after the party. (Metal probably won't go to the party anyway, unless it's an opening for establishing their ambitions.)

For sexual harmony

Keep a window open when you enjoy sexual intimacy indoors. This brings beneficial spirals of energy into the Metal/Wood relationship. Make sure the bed faces north if possible. If not, paint the walls in Water colours – shades of blue or inky black – as a contrast with a hot Fire colour such as deep fuchsia pink or geranium red. Water cures are essential in this sexual relationship to allow better communication and energy to flow between you. Make love in the shower or the bath – frequently! This can inspire Metal's sense of eroticism and Wood's need for cool detachment. Wood people are experimenters and Metal are more conventional, so take the middle road and enjoy lovemaking in an environment that has been harmonized with incense and candles. Use citrus-scented incense and red or black candles for erotic energy. Warm up your emotions with Fire, either by enjoying the sun on your back in the great outdoors or by placing a piece of Carnelian beside your bed. Mirrors are an invaluable enhancement to this relationship.

Use mirrors for vitalizing energy, and paint the frames black. If you can, get hold of a double-sided mirror and angle it so that one side reflects the light from the south and the other the north. Simplicity is the key to a successful liaison, so make sure you keep the bed covered in soft fabrics and velvet cushions. Add some glamorous silk or satin to vitalize your sense of touch, and for dynamic passion paint a green dragon above your doorway.

Metal/Earth

'To wake the soul by tender strokes of art . . . '

These are two elements which can get their act together without much trouble. Both are instinctively tuned into their own needs, and each may at times alarm the other with a selfish or inflexible streak. However, Metal people quickly learn to express their sexual energy via the sensual and receptive arms of Earth. Persistence may pay off in the bedroom for Earth, when Metal seems at times unwilling to go with the flow. Together they provide each other with sexual support and romantic intensity that can't easily be invaded once established.

A blend of awareness and vision means that love can become a powerful and evolving scenario for this combination. Sexual energy gathers with a mutual need for practical basics and an ability to sense each other's seductive qualities. A slow and careful build-up of feeling and intensity can make this the perfect physical partnership.

Earth is the supreme sensualist and Metal the extreme eroticist. Earth can easily ensure the magnitude of Metal's inflexible sexual attitude because the two elements share the need for self-gratification within their own boundaries. The most stimulating aspect of their love-making will be that they each feel safe knowing who they are and where their hearts lie.

For sexual harmony

Use the subtle hues of Water colours in your room, with turquoise, jade and duck-egg blue soft sheen paints to enhance your communication and imagination. Passion becomes inflaming rather than engulfing when you choose vibrant red or yellow fabrics or fantasy paintings to bring missing Fire into your interior landscape. Images of waterfalls, fountains and rainbows, as subtle additions in the form of objects, photos or paintings will ensure positive audacity in what might otherwise be an introspective relationship.

New positions, new ideas, role-changing – the sense of change and discovery is an important element here. Be first to suggest a different game, light up some scented candles, particularly those with heady, exotic perfumes such as cinnabar, sandalwood or patchouli. Stimulate your senses and forget about your money or business worries. Earth/Metal combinations often spend more time discussing how to manage their business and financial affairs than their own passionate involvement.

To bring something totally new into your sexual experimentation, try making love on a bed of crisp ten-pound notes (if you haven't got that much cash lying around, use Monopoly money!) – this could be the ultimate turn-on for Metal/Earth passion.

The Fire that needs to rage eternal for this combination needs stoking occasionally, or it can turn inward and become elusive. Bring reds into your bed in the form of silk or satin sheets, rich operatic or film score music, and mirrors that reflect the sunrise. Think French hot nights, red lights and red wine, rather than cool linens and chilled white wine. These enriching cures can be incorporated to enhance the missing qualities of flexibility and potency. Place a piece of Amber on your windowsill to draw away any difficult energy, and a piece of Amethyst near your bed for complete surrender.

Metal/Water

'What potions have I drunk of Siren tears . . . '

This is a relationship that is sparkling in its energy level, and yet can blow a fuse if you aren't aware of the different and challenging feelings involved.

Although Metal and Water both feel their path through life, they do so in very different ways. Water is romantic and sensitive to every mood change around, while Metal is astute at recognizing such atmospheres. But Metal maintains its own flow, while Water goes with the flow. See the difference?

For Water, Metal is probably the partner who can best inspire a sexual adventure into the unknown. Metal needs to overwhelm and to be thoroughly involved in every second of sexual intensity. Emotionally they may appear cold, but their deeper instincts are the kind that Water can bring to the surface. Water people are not deep-sea divers; their light and ephemeral quality is more that of mermaids and mermen, those who can live deep in the ocean and yet be at home in the air.

Water's transient needs in bed can be disturbing to the more dedicated and compulsive style of Metal, yet this very inconsistency in Water's sexuality may prove to be a challenge that is irresistible for Metal.

For sexual harmony

Night time and the darkness is an erotic atmosphere for this combination. Make sure the beds and furniture have no hard edges to disturb the currents of Ch'i. Use soft colours such as pistachio, peppermint and almond blossom, lavender, sage green or the incredible blue of cornflowers; billowing muslin curtains, flowing fabrics like voile and silk on the bed; plants that grow upwards rather than trail. Strong lines of tall cacti or fast-growing rubber plants are ideal. The energy of plants growing upwards will help you focus on evolving sexuality rather than static visions. Trailing plants can drag your energy down, disturbing for the highly sensitive Water and depressing for Metal.

Play the vamp; dress in exotic underwear or erotic clothes – anything to take the strain out of the moods and vibrations of this unusual relationship. Ensure that Metal sleeps on the left of the bed and that Water either gets some ear-plugs or falls into a deep sleep before Metal decides it's time to do a replay. Metal is highly sexed, don't forget! This relationship can generate unpredictable behaviour in and out of the bed, so make it more clandestine and more secretive. Make love in weird places and you could soon find this pair have the most outrageous of ideas, for Water is clever and Metal is inventive.

It may be necessary to bring in missing Wood and Earth in the form of natural discoveries such as fossils or stones.

An excellent enhancement for this combination is bed coverings or fabrics that have a 'crackled' design like tie dyed fabrics. This sort of pattern is an ancient Chinese cure for vitalizing male sexuality. If the mind was energized, the performance would be potent and creative! Finally, place a piece of Azurite near the bed to clear away old memories and energy that may be clouding either head or heart.

Water/Water

'A dealer in magic and spells . . . '

Because of the inconsistent nature of two Water elements, together there is often an intangible quality to this relationship that others may find hard to stomach. With such changeable natures and imaginative dreams, sex for these two can become airy and insubstantial, rather than the grounded reality that is the result of more erotic contact.

Because both partners are equally talented at picking up on each other's moods, they may find it difficult to decide whose feelings are whose. But at times when one is passive and the other is active they can swop roles and enjoy romantic fantasies rich in escapist elements.

For sexual harmony

Magic is an intrinsic part of the energy that flows between two Water elements. Use unusual lighting or shutters instead of curtains, an orgy of muslin draped across the bed or those oriental paper blinds that allow a flicker of sunlight into the love-nest. Water people often prefer the crystal light of daytime love-making. Changing moods keep Water lovers on their toes, yet can be conflicting when you are both feeling equally neurotic. Water people sometimes find it excruciatingly hard to convince themselves they exist at all.

Your responses will quicken and your sexual energy will flow best when you are surrounded by music, or sounds which bring harmony to your ears. Avoid living or sleeping under a flight path as it will disturb the intuitive pathway you both use to connect with your deeper underlying passion. If you have no choice, place a piece of Amber in your bedroom to draw up the vibrational energies that may block your sexual responses. Wood cures should be incorporated to remind you of the reality of the natural world. Find a piece of driftwood or a carved wooden statue and pile some books in the Fire area of your bedroom.

Try to keep your bed facing forests, woods or trees, or distant gardens or parks if you live in the middle of the city. If this is impossible, bring images of forests, landscapes or plants into your bedroom. Use imaginative dream paintings, fake fur fabrics and unusual antique or modern objets d'art to lull you into a relaxed mood.

Water finds it difficult to let go of the tensions and problems of everyday life, and so the calmer and more serene the atmosphere the better. Quiet secluded places, white decor and soft glittering silver and gold fabrics will bring successful eroticism into your relationship, and lots of red and green candles will introduce the calmness of Wood and the passion of Fire. Make sure you keep some doors open to release any still pools of stagnant energy. Water can drown in its own murky depths and pull a few others down with it. To keep you both physically and emotionally flexible, incorporate paintings or photos that evoke flowing water.

Choose a landscape of a mountain stream or a scene of mythological passions to stir Fire into both your hearts.

Water/Fire

'Dissolve me into ecstasies.'

There is no easy flow of energy here, as these elements represent passionate dynamism versus sensitivity. But Water and Fire can produce some pretty steamy stuff if they are sure they can handle the different styles of loving and living that each has to offer. Fire may well become quickly infatuated by Water's deeply responsive approach to physical love. This is of course to Fire's advantage. The more someone else responds to Fire's advances and dissolves into their demanding passion, the less Fire has to think about anyone else's needs. Perhaps Water already knows how to handle Fire.

At the outset Fire's enthusiasm is so hot that Water will enjoy the fireworks and go with the flow. But Fire likes to leap into the future too fast and may find Water gets tired of the pace. Fire may also be jealous of Water's ability to listen to every other person's problems in great depth and to empathize with the whole world, when Fire needs to be the centre of attention at all times. Sexually, Fire hasn't got time for games or devices, while Water would rather take imagination to its limits and be unpredictable and capricious.

Water types are natural listeners but never give much away themselves. They are excellent healers but can turn into victims and martyrs if they haven't faced the music of their own inner self. Fire, on the other hand, demands to know exactly what is going on in their partner's head at all times. The passion of Fire may find it hard to invade the deeper feelings and emotions of Water's sexual ambivalence, because Water people are quite unaware of it themselves.

For sexual harmony

Avoid bringing more Fire into the home. Candles are fine but don't use red ones. Too many mirrors may make Water feel they're drowning in Fire's enthusiasm. Impulsive Fire may find that Water's need to escape and avoid scenes is incredibly frustrating, but also a big tease. For Fire, of course, anything that is hard to come by makes for good sex.

Ensure that you have Earth and Wood in your bedroom to keep the conversation going into the small hours and then you'll both be drooling for different reasons. Wood can be incorporated with a four-poster bed if you've got the finances to support one. If not, hang up posters, photos or paintings of trees and forests. Paint a jungle mural behind your bed to remind you of the 'Beauty and the Beast' quality of nature. Earth and Wood are easily integrated into the bedroom via furniture; but try to find pieces that have curved edges to allow beneficial energy to travel freely around your room.

Strong terracottas and simple vegetable or fruity colours such as mulberry, sage green and ochre will enable Fire and Water to vitalize their different energies. If you hate this kind of colour scheme, start a library instead. Books are not such obvious Wood cures, but placed beneath the bed or on a shelf beneath the window, they can empower the room with more liberal energy. Use your imagination and fantasize together, or have sexual adventures in different places to avoid the same old scenario. For Water this is particularly important as boredom and routine are the stop-cocks (no pun intended) to their true sexual flow. Remember, Fire has the nerve and the verve to get away with anything, and Water has the imagination.

An excellent cure to enable Water and Fire to inspire each other is to put a small piece of Jade or Smoky Quartz in a velvet bag and place it under your pillow while you sleep.

Water/Wood

'He went back through the Wet, Wild Woods, waving his wild tail . . . But he never told anybody.'

This is what I suppose one could call a valuable sexual relationship. Water and Wood are conscious of other people's needs in different ways, but because they share awareness and poise and both prefer to be uninvolved rather than possessed, this can often lead to a partnership that matures with time rather like a good Brie. Sexually they relate well to each other's somewhat cool approach. Wood's fear of intimacy feels comfortable and relaxed in the laid-back arms of Water, and Water can drift along with Wood's ambivalence without fear of being thrust into a corner with a spotlight shining in their face. Being put on the spot about sex is difficult for Water because Water people can't quite make up their minds who they are and what they want. Wood may be idealistic about relationships, but usually prefers to assume responsibility for who's on top, where, when and how. Water's great insight and intuition mean that they are always prepared for any unusual twists or changes of direction in their physical bonding. Water instinctively knows that Wood people have to expand their sexual knowledge. Water/Wood is a powerful intuitive connection.

There is a good blend of elements here for yummy sexual harmony, but the addition of Earth and Metal can supplement a pleasurable experience with a few twists and turns to counteract any traces of boredom.

For sexual harmony

A good way to augment missing Earth, without feeling tied down and committed, is to use the sensual indulgence of aromatherapy, especially if you choose natural oils from plants. Your skin needs stimulus because your head works overtime as it is, so to add more movement to the exterior surfaces of your body, sink into a scented bath and then into luxurious pillows and sheets. Silk or satin are great for getting the feelings to flow and, if you've got the nose for it, plenty of incense or exotic smelly candles will help to incorporate missing Fire.

Make sure your windows face open skies so that you can see the moon and the stars rather than someone else's garage roof. If you can't, then paint stars on your ceiling. Don't live in a basement if you can help it, and ensure your neighbours aren't polluting the environment with noise – radios and cars starting up at 6 a.m. are not good for the vibrations of Wood and Water. If you do live in a basement, the best cure is to place Green Tourmaline in the Core area of your home. This stone is a bridge builder between heaven and earth, and has a powerful protective energy. If you can't move away from your noisy neighbours, use Lapis Lazuli in your Core area. Avoid metal furniture as this element must be used carefully by Wood and Water lovers. Don't forget, Metal is about autonomy – all for one, not one for all – and it could upset Wood's visions of universal peace. Used with subtle sophistication (a Wood virtue) Metal can enrich this most responsive and aesthetic of relationships. Try silver and gold threads hung from the end of your bed, or silver chains strung across a gilt-framed painting.

Water/Earth

'I hope I didn't intrude?'

Earth people have a problem living in the realms of imagination, fantasy and illusion, and in accepting the unpredictable. They prefer to trust the forces of energy and the meaning of natural life. Earth people need consistency and staying power in their sexual expression. Knowing where you are and where you are going is about stability, nurturing and sensual, grounded sex. However, Water doesn't have much to do with tangibles and prefers the romance and the dream to linger longer than even Earth can stand for all their stamina! These two together are sometimes like clay on a potter's wheel. As the centrifugal force of Water gathers momentum, the particles of Earth's reality spin into shape and mould a joint destiny based on different elemental blends. But there are times when they can become like a muddy pond in summer that's shrinking round the sides and about to dry up.

Your energy flow may border on the stagnant if you don't allow time to communicate your true feelings. Water needs to flow and Earth needs to feel physically moved. Water has an extraordinary desire to play games and to seduce, whereas Earth likes to get down to basics and enjoy simple erotic body contact. If you're Earth, you need your senses to be aroused, rather than your emotions which can become tangled up like seaweed in Water's moods and inconsistent escapades.

For sexual harmony

If Earth and Water can understand each other's different needs, they may become the hand-crafted pot of the potter's wheel. To keep the wheel turning, music can be literally the food of love-making in this relationship. Sexual energy between you may be kept in motion with sensitive background music; wind chimes are a must, or a tape of hump-backed whales mating!

A low bed keeps Water grounded and Earth closer to it. You may carry each other away over a candlelit dinner, but watch out that emotions don't get out of hand when Water just wants the candle-smoke to cloud their eyes and Earth would rather get down to an intimate embrace before the end of the first course. Earth may well point out that dreams are for when you're sleeping.

Incorporate Fire into your energy field with an open fire and, if you haven't got one, pretend. Use candles, smouldering incense or warm, red and dusky lighting. Place your best candles all over the room and sometimes make lighting them part of your love-making scenario. Try using Metal to keep you both aware of each other's rhythms. Silver and gold should be used with caution but can be incorporated in bed fabrics and as mirror surrounds. You don't need refinement, you need dedication. Choose earthy metals, wrought iron chandeliers, or bronze or pewter goblets to hold your scented candles. Stand an unusual metal sculpture on your window ledge, and a piece of Malachite or even a White Quartz crystal in your undies drawer to inspire you every time you open it.

Fire/Fire

'Fire! Fire! Fire! Fire! Pour on Water, pour on Water . . . '

A bucket or two of Water is unlikely to have much effect on two Fire elements when they are hot for each other. Imagine a forest blaze that burns so quickly that nothing can keep up with its breathtaking energy and speed. Falling in love can be a sudden and impulsive experience for two Fire people, and their passions are so volatile that it doesn't take long for them both to be ransacking the sexual library of discovery for something new every time they meet or make love.

The strength of Fire is their initiative and the audacious way they are able to begin romance, evoke passion and activate sexual pleasure. Their weakness (for two doses of one element together often produces too much of a good thing) arises because they are both headstrong and impatient so there may come a time when one gets restless and impulsively falls for someone totally different, just for the challenge. Yet while still in the flames of desire they'll stoke each other up like a roaring sexual furnace and make it virtually impossible for anyone else to break down their relationship. Fire people always know where they want to go in love, and what they want next from sexual fantasy, but it can take them a long time to arrive. Their urgency leads to many changes in sexual direction as they provoke one another into physical oneupmanship.

Fire needs fantasy first and deep emotional contact very rarely or not at all. Fire and Fire can arouse each other splendidly by opting for daring places in which to make love, and using words and gestures (erotic phone calls, for example) which turn them both on like electricity. Their nature is exuberant, so if you are Fire involved with another Fire element then enjoy the fun and games, because there is little to beat this up-tempo combination.

For sexual harmony

Missing Earth must be incorporated to ground the more volatile side of your relationship. Make sure you live near trees, or at least have some pot plants in your bedroom if that's where you enjoy most of your sexual activity. You're both extravagant and passionate in your sexual performance. To enhance your flexibility and sensitivity, fill a glass bowl with water and place shells or coloured bits of glass in the water to vitalize the essence of the ocean in your energy field. Try to have your bed facing south if you can. If not, hang a mirror on the south-facing wall to reflect the purity of sunlight into your home. Keep curtains open and use white candles and silver-edged mirrors to augment Metal. You both have a need to be on top, literally, in sexual positions and in your relationship, so you might have to make a few compromises about who comes first in bed, as well as who makes breakfast. Food is a wonderful ingredient to add to your sexual adventures. To ensure a more sensual approach to your lovemaking, go camping in the big outdoors and stew some beans over a pile of logs. A taste of Earth keeps you in touch with the vastness of nature. Place a bowl of peaches, figs and apricots in your bedroom, or eat pine nuts and oysters as a food elixir and an aphrodisiac.

Massaging each other is a wonderful precursor to a night of passion, and the more exotic the oils or smells with which you surround yourself the more likely it is that you will keep the anticipation going. It's important to keep Fire's potency alive and kicking. Your flames can burn up so fast that the great sexual crescendo is over and done with before you've got time to blink. Fire loves fantasy, so read each other erotic stories in bed – a good bedside library is essential!

Fire/Earth

'With taper light to seek the beauteous eye . . . '

Although quite dissimilar in their energy flow and basic needs and values in life, somehow this strange mixture of optimism and caution can kindle a passionate little smoulder. Like autumn leaves crackling on the bonfire, the magic of the aroma can run deep. Fire and Earth are awfully good at fuelling each other's desires.

Earth's sensuality is important here, for although Earth people may tire of Fire's speedy desires and childlike sexual antics, they'll be fascinated by the courage and daring of Fire's extraordinary imagination. Earth can provide a deeply sexual and reliable relationship, one where Fire can take off to the realms of fantasy without alarming anyone, certainly not the grounded serenity of Earth. Pleasant stimulation rather than emotional intensity is the style of this odd pairing. But their energy does need boosting, not because Fire lacks it, but because Earth people can sometimes make Fire feel impatient and frustrated when their entanglements between the sheets are not at the tempo Fire would prefer.

For sexual harmony

It might be best for these two to do a lot of their love-making out of doors. Earth will appreciate communing with nature, and Fire will love the thrill of anywhere which is different. The more varied and dangerous the locations for sex, the more Fire will let Earth control the performance. Both can get something out of this deeply erotic link-up. A few books on Tantric sex could also enhance their love-making and bring in the essence of Metal energy as a harmonizing balance. (Metal is about control, and Tantric sex is basically about control of orgasm through yoga and breathing.)

Better avoid having sex in water, unless you can turn the shower off quickly! Water could be damaging to your sexual performance and your psyche. If you're Fire, learn to use your headstrong passion to sensualize Earth rather than rushing to adopt a new position or a change of routine at every liaison. This is why it's essential to incorporate a Wood cure. One of the best cures for Earth and Fire is to place a piece of Onyx under your bed. This both grounds your awareness and brings stability.

To vitalize sexual desire, keep your clothes on for as long as possible, or all the time, and don't bother with fetishes or sexy underwear. The purer and the more idealistic you are about sex, the more you may enjoy it. Wood can be brought into your surroundings with carved figures, or perhaps a four-poster. Climbing rather than trailing plants may be placed on window ledges, and you should choose furniture with curved edges to keep the flow of beneficial energy spiralling through your heart.

Fire/Wood

'Hunting he loved, but love he laughed to scorn . . . '

This is usually an excellent combination of energies. Together you can create the kind of sexual harmony that many would envy. This is smooth, sophisticated and essentially fluid energy, a blend of coffee and cream that makes your mouth water and reminds you of passionate films and heady romances. Even so, Fire/Wood can have problems like any other combination.

First they should learn to establish their own needs so that they can support each other. This is a volatile mixture of Air and Fire, for Wood feeds Fire and puts Fire's vision and ideals to practical use. Their sexual agendas won't stay hidden for long, with Wood's broad-minded and liberal use of language and sexual ideas and Fire's extraordinary need to get on and do it, whatever it is. What Wood loves about Fire is the way they swing into action without a moment's hesitation. Love and sex are about having fun and enjoying the risks involved in being daring. For Wood's altruistic nature, this can seem like the perfect blend of spirits in a highly sociable setting. Both don't hang too much on the emotional content of their sex life, so they can identify easily with mutual freedom. Extroverts, they thrive on mad and crazy sex, doing it anywhere and everywhere. The notion of adding anything to the environment may just be too much of a drag for Fire, who hasn't got time, while Wood may love the idea but could take all night to work out whether it's worth the effort.

For sexual harmony

Surround yourself with erotic images to liven up your sexual vibrations. Paintings are a must, either wonderfully abstract or black and white erotica, anything cool and lucid, refined and aesthetic. Erotic here means sensual, not porn!

Try out black and yellow fabrics on the bed, metal furniture and sculpture around the room. Metal can help you to focus more clearly on the kind of physical aspiration you both may talk about but sometimes fail to achieve.

Because Fire and Wood often produce a raging inferno together, there are times when you suffocate in the heat. So use the missing Water element in your environment. Try taking a few ice cubes and roll around on the floor with them, slide them down each other's skin and lick off the drips. Alternatively, freeze some champagne and enjoy champagne ice – it tastes better! A glass bowl of coloured water placed where the sunlight can glint on the surface will do wonders to relax you both.

You need humour and invention in your sex life. Indulge in some silly sex aids, rubber knickers or weird and wonderful vibrators to make you laugh. Surround yourselves with a dozen or so white candles and hang muslins over the bed, and floating curtains at the windows. Music can be a powerful cure for straying ideals. Music evokes those feelings you may both prefer to keep hidden, so turn on your favourite concerto and dance before you get too close. This kind of build-up is often more erotic for Fire than the sexual act itself. Wood may fear intimacy and prefer to dance alone, so choose something to reflect desire without giving away your dreams.

Place a White Quartz crystal, or a Diamond if you have one, beneath your window to refract the energy and illuminate the power of your instincts.

Wood/Wood

'And saw . . . an angel writing in a book of gold.'

However far Wood pursues freedom in a relationship there will come the day when someone poses that dreaded question of commitment, unless the other partner is Wood too. This combination works well if both are equally keen to follow their own lives. If both Wood people are pure Wood in the sense that their altruism is genuine and not built on guilt, and their need for freedom allows their partner freedom too, then this blend of idealistic and unpossessive harmony may make an orchestral work out of a nursery rhyme.

The only trouble for Wood/Wood is that because they are both pursuing their own humanitarian goals, they don't have an awful lot of time to spare between the sheets. What attracts them to each other in the first place is the one thing Wood finds difficult to hold on to: romance. These two are born romantics, and they want romance to last for ever. The routine and monotony of physical closeness can spoil that romance, so it's best if these two are separated by work and social necessity as often as possible, so that they can enjoy getting back together after being away and rejoicing in their freedom. Roses round the door and warm slippers by the fire aren't for Wood. Wood people require sophisticated love, in the sense that simplicity is not enough – love must be fashioned and refined, although paradoxically this will never be put into words. For Wood, love must defy sensuality and the purity of sexual desire. It must mean so much more and say so much less.

Wood/Wood have a problem in communicating their needs for they both fear to reveal too much of their souls.

Wood would rather fly with the wind and trade bodies for wisdom! If you are Wood you may understand this airy need to scatter your ideals on as many journeys as you can. For two Wood elements together, there can be an unstated agreement, an intuitive knowing that whatever the other does or however the other acts, it's OK to be like that.

Excellent at seducing, at making love and knowing how to play every game in the book, Wood is always seeking an ideal. Talk is their unadulterated passion. Perhaps their greatest union can be enjoyed over a game of Scrabble or on the telephone. Conversation is highly arousing to the Wood psyche even though they fear discussing their feelings. They have a deep connection through abstract understanding, but it is still important to get out and feel the earth move!

For sexual harmony

For a creative sex life you need natural visual stimuli. Make sure your bed faces the window and you can see trees, hills, rivers or lakes. If you can't get a view of the park or even the garden from your bedroom, the best cure to bring sensuality into your sex life is a glass jar of fossils, shells or pebbles placed beneath your bed, or on a low shelf beside it. These stimulate the Earth energy that may be difficult for you both to invoke. If you live in a city, use your inspiration to get out into the country – go camping and make love under the stars.

Decorate your bedroom in simple colours – whites and creams or duck-egg blue and coral – to ground and refine your sexual energy and give you a better sense of your own needs. Use dramatic Metal sculptures or gilt-framed pictures. Gold is a valuable energizer for eternal romantics, so paint gold designs on your walls, bring in bedcovers or curtains with gold thread and for sheer indulgence hang a huge gilt-framed mirror that reflects the daylight. Place a bonsai tree on the windowsill as a cure for being obsessed with having perfect sex every time you make love! Grounded sex is essential, so if you live on the tenth floor of a block of flats choose the floorboards rather than the bed as another inspiration for vitalizing your sexual energy. To maximize your sexual harmony place Rose Quartz beneath your pillow during the day, and at night, or when sleeping, place it near the window.

Wood/Earth

'If you'll believe in me, I'll believe in you.'

The guarded yet discriminating energy of Earth is not exactly the kind of love that Wood searches for in their freedom quest. Wood is essentially outgoing and flexible, while Earth people are dogmatic, receptive and prefer to be chased rather than to do any chasing themselves. Wood may wander into Earth's territory without intending to get involved, merely doing what Wood does best, which is searching for universal truths about life and love. Confronting a charming sensualist such as Earth can be enlightening. And opposites, for all their conflicts, are often magnetically fascinated by their differences.

If Wood can cope with the emotional undercurrents of Earth's tenacity, both can share erotic bliss and sexual ecstasy – if, and only if, Wood really wants this in the first place. Wood knows instinctively how Earth feels and can soak up Earth's moods and indulgences only too easily. But

Wood's grand visions and ideals and their desire to merge into the universal meaning of existence can destroy Earth's need to be a receptor too, but on a one-to-one basis. Socially Earth and Wood move in different circles, so it may be that as a couple they would find it difficult to harmonize their needs except when between the sheets. Even then it can prove tricky. Earth wants eroticism, while Wood may just want to think and dream about it. Earth people can withdraw deeply into themselves and Wood would prefer not to get too close to Earth's hidden self, let alone their own – so the conflict of their inner images is a strong one. Yet the way they physically channel this energy can be brought into a wonderful pulse of throbbing passion, if Earth's sluggish nature gets enough of a jolt from the wide-ranging sexual exploits of Wood.

For sexual harmony

Food is a valuable resource for you to energize your sexual Ch'i. Enjoy dinner in bed, breakfast in bed, anything in bed (or a picnic under the stars) as long as you share it! Sprinkle each other with sherbet lemon, and use your imagination to choose which end of your lover's body to start licking it from. Have a bath in the deepest bubbles with a bottle of wine by your side. Water is an essential element to balance you both, and so sex under water, in the bath, in the shower or in the sea is highly beneficial. Invest in a waterbed if the idea gives you a buzz. Make sure your bed faces east and that you can see the stars from your pillow, or at least a chink of sky. Don't encourage too much Metal into your home as this is destructive for Wood. But Earth responds very well to Metal, so if you feel that Metal could draw Earth away from materialism, add silver or gold wind chimes to your love-nest.

You also need music and the sounds of waterfalls or streams. Fountains could be a big turn-on! Keep a jug of water under your bed or on a window ledge, and don't be surprised how quickly it evaporates in the heat of this relationship. Fire can energize you both in the right places, so bring in some incense or candles. Use red ones for inflaming passion and dark blue or black ones to add a touch of magic when you're feeling completely in tune. Use reds and deep midnight blues or inky charcoal and black in fabrics and wall coverings to add the mystique of romance and adventure to every sexual encounter. For connecting and vitalizing your energy so that it flows from day to day, place a piece of Amethyst in your bedroom where the sunlight can animate the crystal's quality of trust and enhance your awareness of each other's needs.

Earth/Earth

'I cried, "Come tell me how you live!" and
thumped him on the head.'

To an outsider, the erotic nature of this partnership can seem overwhelmingly intense. Yet for two Earth-dominated people there is little doubt in their minds, or their bodies for that matter, that physical blending and mutual sensuality get top billing. Both are highly in tune with the other's needs, so sexually they can perhaps find compatibility faster than any other element combination. They ground sexuality into a purpose, and the pleasuring of their bodies is mutual. Love is a sticky kind of word for Earth. It doesn't quite mean sex, but when they are having sex they are usually making love. The only real problem for two Earth lovers is that they need to be touched and they can become dependent on that touch for their own sense of self-worth. Caution becomes a key word in their sexual vocabulary and the desire to be inventive, spontaneous and risky often loses its impetus when Earth/Earth hold back, just in case they make fools of themselves.

Loving nature so much means that nudity and the body are taken as beautiful without question. The urge to vanish into the woods may not be a sudden impulse. Instead, ideas will be planned and put carefully into action. Picnics in the park can turn into a sensual delight, and furtive looks and secret touches and responses in company remind both Earth people that their seductive quality can inspire others as well as themselves. This can lead to jealousy and, unfortunately, Earth is possessive. But for all their consistency and persistence, Earth/Earth can turn an emotional reaction into a sexual performance before they've had time to close the curtains!

For sexual harmony

Music is essential, so take a CD player or a radio into your bedroom. Ensure you have plenty of Water in your surroundings too. If you can't quite cope with a bubbling fish tank, use images or paintings depicting waterfalls, oceans, rivers or even rain. Other good Water cures can be incorporated using shells, fossils and tropical fish images. Colour can also play an enhancing part, so paint the walls in deep inky colours if you dare, or use velvet curtains and dark sumptuous fabrics for your bed. Bring Fire into your environment to add sparkle and spontaneity to your love-making with mirrors anywhere where you can see yourselves. However, don't have mirrors reflecting you as you sleep, as this is one way of draining your inner energies. Keep the mirror on a wall that reflects the sunlight from the window, or the doorway. Cover the bed with mock furs in winter, or silk sheets in summer. Use blacks, greens and purples and fill the room with antiques and Metal objets d'art or sculptures. To bring a lighter, airier quality to your sexual connection, hang muslins and gauzy curtains at the windows to let the moonlight shimmer and blend with your softest and most sensual music. For a complete sexual enhancer, use a piece of Azurite to clear away the past and bring you to the threshold of inspiring love.

Chapter Ten

How to Balance a Two-home Relationship

Whether you have established a long-term relationship and you live in separate homes, or you've just met the love of your life and haven't yet decided to commit yourselves to living together, this chapter takes you down another pathway towards working out which part of your home may be in need of harmony. If your partner is interested in creating harmony in his/her home too, you can each use this pathway separately (but if your partner isn't too keen on the idea, don't force it). Creating harmony in your love life doesn't necessarily depend on your other half, although it can enrich your lives if you both choose to do so. However, if you try to force someone else into practising Feng Shui in their own home, you may well cause more problems than were there in the first place.

If your partner becomes enthusiastic about Feng Shui and if you both do the following exercise, with different results, do what is right for each of you in your own homes. Don't try to alter your partner's personal perception of his/

her relationship with you. And remember, if you both need to create harmony in the same area of the Bagua, this doesn't necessarily mean the same room in each of your homes.

The magic square numbers

Numbers are symbolic in both Chinese mysticism and our own European methods of divination. In the Bagua they represent powerful energies that have been translated into words through numbers. The magic square is just that: magic!

4	9	2
3	5	7
8	1	6

Figure 22: The magic square. Which of the words below sums up your relationship now? Add your own word to the list if necessary.

Passionate	Volatile	Insecure
Sexual	Static	Relaxed
Erotic	Dull	Free
Stimulating	Bored	Confused
Transforming	Restless	Committed

With the magic square in Figure 22 in front of you, look at the list of words with it, and decide which *one* word sums up your relationship right now. By using the code in Figure 23 (an ancient symbolic key for letters and numbers), add up the numbers of each letter in your word so that you end up with one simple number between 1 and 9. For example, if the word you chose was 'passionate', then $7+1+1+1+9+6+5+1+2+5 = 38$; then $3+8 = 11$; and $1+1 = 2$. So the number 2 is important to your relationship now.

Figure 23: Pythagorean system of numbers.

1	2	3	4	5	6	7	8	9
A	B	C	D	E	F	G	H	I
J	K	L	M	N	O	P	Q	R
S	T	U	V	W	X	Y	Z	

However, in Feng Shui, the place where you live is also a part of who you are. If you live in a building which has its own number, you must include this as well. For example, if you live at 12, High Street, reduce this to a single number: $1+ 2 = 3$.

If you live in a bedsit or flat use the number of the flat, but also the number of the building if it has one. For example, you may live at Flat 2, 32 Surrey Road: $2+3+2 = 7$.

If you live at an address where you have no number but your house has a name, use that instead. For example, if you lived in Peartree Cottage you would have to add all the letters of PEARTREE COTTAGE together.

Next add your own personal number, which is derived

from your date of birth. For example, if you were born on 15 October 1962, you would add 1+5+10 (October is the tenth month) +1+9+6+2 = 34; then 3+4 = 7.

Finally, add this 7 to your house or street number, and also your specially chosen word number. Add them all together until you reduce the total to a single digit number. This final number is the area of the magic square you should be concentrating on at the moment.

Now place the Bagua map over your home and see which room or area this number on the Bagua relates to. Look back to Figure 3A on page 24 if you can't remember which number relates to which of the Bagua energies.

If your partner has also completed the magic square exercise, you may find you have to concentrate on different areas in your respective homes – or you may find they match, whether it's the same number or in the same room. Whatever the case, if you are both creating harmony you should attempt to use similar remedies. If you are doing this alone because your partner isn't interested, then enjoy placing the cure for both of you.

Cures for the magic number exercise

If your number is 1
Corresponds to Bagua area Water

If you can, place a mirror on the wall which faces south in this area of your home. Use lush glowing lights and paintings that remind you of summer heatwaves, photos of volcanoes or a real bronze statue beside your doorway. If you want to use a cure in your bedroom, find where your Water area is by placing the Bagua over a plan of your bedroom and, to create deeper harmony, light a scented candle or 'opium-scented' incense whenever there is a new moon.

If your number is 2
Corresponds to Bagua area Earth

If possible, place a mirror on the wall that faces north-east in this area of your home. Wind chimes are indispensable here; if you can, use those that are made of wood, as muted tones are especially auspicious. For extra vitality and to ensure good friendship, place a piece of Malachite beneath a window where it can refract the sunlight.

If your number is 3
Corresponds to Bagua area Thunder

Particularly if this area is in your bedroom, hang a mirror on the wall that faces west. Silver and gold can be incorporated by using gilt-framed pictures, or by hanging silver necklaces, rings and bangles from any hook or doorknob. For special and long-lasting magic, incorporate a Tree of Life design as a painting or print (or on a bedspread if this is your bedroom area). These designs can often be found in oriental shops and at markets. Alternatively, use a succulent such as a 'money plant' or a bonsai tree.

If your number is 4
Corresponds to Bagua area Wind

If possible, hang a mirror on the wall of this area that faces north-west. Use a wooden sculpture, or piece of carved furniture if you can. Stand incense sticks in a wooden jug, or a white candle in a wooden candlestick. Light these whenever there is a full moon. Have something green in this room; one of the most harmonizing remedies, if you can find one, is a green dragon – either a painting or one of those papier-mâché models you can buy at markets.

If your number is 5
Corresponds to Bagua area Core

This is a splendid part of the home in which to harmonize those deeper energies of your relationship, so bring the biggest and most inspiring candles you can find into this area. If possible use two candle sconces and hang them on opposite walls. It doesn't matter which way they face as long as they are in polarity to each other. Use white or, if you can get them, silver or gold candles. Apart from this energizer, keep this area special and ensure that there isn't too much furniture in the room.

If your number is 6
Corresponds to Bagua area Heaven

If you can, place a mirror on the wall that faces south-east. One of the most beautiful cures for harmonizing this environment is to hang a piece of Selenite from the window frame directly in the light. This superb stone is a great energizer for telepathic insight and connects you to your partner. If you can't find any, use White Quartz crystal but choose a piece that is pointed at both ends – the energy of these crystals is doubly strengthened for intuitive communication.

If your number is 7
Corresponds to Bagua area Lake

A sensual area to harmonize and one that needs serenity. Choose a convex, round or oval mirror rather than a square or oblong. Hang it on the wall that faces east if you can. Again, this area benefits from a crystal hung in the window; use Rose Quartz for pure unselfish love or Pink Tourmaline to activate your feelings and deeper desires.

If your number is 8
Corresponds to Bagua area Mountain

This area can be energized by placing a mirror on the wall that faces south-west. A valuable source of energy here can be incorporated with a bowl or stone vessel filled with pebbles or unpolished tiny crystals in the colour or variety of your choice. Place the bowl on the floor where it can receive both sunlight and, if possible, moonlight, to draw in the flow of the natural planetary rhythms and cycles.

If your number is 9
Corresponds to Bagua area Fire

This area undoubtedly needs careful handling so ensure you first place a candle sconce (or a mirror with a candle in front of it) on the wall that faces north. Use a vibrant colour scheme behind your mirror and candle, such as a red, purple or gold wallhanging or tapestry or a piece of heavy fabric. Another wonderful vitalizer for this area is to place a White Quartz crystal and a Carnelian together on a surface where they can receive the daylight and channel their own perfect harmony.

Chapter Eleven

Solving Problems

Here are some ways of using Feng Shui to solve any problems you may have, whether you are single or in a relationship.

The simplest way to find out which area of your home may be the source of a problem is to do the cat spiral first mentioned in the Introduction. Imagine you're a lost cat looking for your home. The way a cat does this, if you remember, is by setting off in an ever-widening circle or spiral until it recognizes its own territory. This can take months or even years. I've had several cats who've disappeared, one of whom, a Siamese, was gone for over a year before he turned up at our old house only two miles away. He'd come across the old energy centre and territory he knew, but it had taken fourteen months for his spiral to get him there.

For you, the spiral route will be incredibly quick because we're going to cheat. First, imagine yourself at the point in Figure 24 where the cat is lost, in other words at the centre of the Bagua map. If you were a real cat you would have to travel round all the nine Bagua energies until you reached home, and for some of us this could take a long time. Instead

I've devised this quick cat spiral connection to the Bagua so that you can move instantly to the area of your home that is most in need of attention and change.

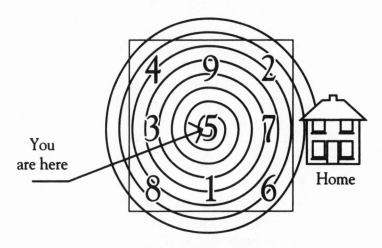

Figure 24: Cat spiral.

Ask yourself the following questions and decide which ones are most significant for you at this time:

1 Have you just split up with your partner? (They left you? You left them? Was it mutual?)

2 Have you just fallen out of love?

3 Are your needs more important than your lover's needs?

4 Are your lover's needs more important than yours?

5 Do you find it difficult to talk to each other?

6 Is your sexual relationship stagnant?

7 Are you suspicious there may be someone else?

8 Are you involved in a love triangle yourself, or deceiving your partner in some way?

9 Do you feel trapped?

10 Does commitment terrify you?

11 Do you want commitment and your partner doesn't?

12 Do you constantly fight about money?

13 Are money, possessions or work big issues and/or sources of conflict in your relationship?

14 Are you overshadowed by family power?

15 Do you find you would rather talk to your mother than to your lover/partner?

16 Do you always seem to meet the wrong types?

17 Do you have many short-term lovers/partners or one-night stands?

18 Are you lonely, lost and confused?

19 Do you want to have children?

20 Are you single and bored?

21 Does your career conflict with your relationship/ love life?

22 Are there any skeletons in the closet that you fear may destroy your relationship?

Have a look at the chart in Figure 25 to discover the area of the Bagua to which your questions relate. Anything you answer 'yes' to corresponds to an area of your home that may be a source of difficulty. If you answer more than one yes, see what they have in common – perhaps they relate to the same area of the Bagua. Focus on the question which seems to push itself out at you right *now*. If you don't answer yes to any of these questions, maybe you just need to brighten up your love-making or revitalize a good grounded relationship. Alternatively, if you feel there is something missing from your love life, turn to the next chapter.

Figure 25: Cat spiral chart.

Questions	Bagua Area	Questions	Bagua Area
1	Water 1	12	Wind 4
2	Thunder 3	13	Wind 4
3	Mountain 8	14	Thunder 3
4	Mountain 8	15	Earth 2
5	Mountain 8	16	Earth 2
6	Lake 7	17	Lake 7
7	Thunder 3	18	Earth 2
8	Thunder 3	19	Fire 9
9	Wind 4	20	Heaven 6
10	Wind 4	21	Heaven 6
11	Water 1	22	Fire 9

Now that you know which area of the Bagua you must work with, place it over the plan of your home to see where you might have to make changes. The following section explains how to restore its balance and harmony to a problem area. Do read the first section about outside the home because, even though your problem area may be centred indoors, if the external situation isn't equally auspicious you may find that making changes inside just isn't enough.

Outside first

In traditional Feng Shui the outside of the house, particularly the bit in front of your main door and the garden and fence at the entrance to your domain, is very important. This area is called the Red Bird and it is highly auspicious – if you get it right.

First, is your house, room or flat at the end of a road, for example, the end of a cul-de-sac? Second, do you have a road, street or path directly pointing at your house? (See Figures 26 and 27.) If your home is sited in such a position then you may have to take immediate steps to instigate a cure. All that energy directed straight down the road towards you is not very kindly! In Feng Shui this kind of Ch'i is called 'secret arrow' – and these are arrows we want kept well away from our house!

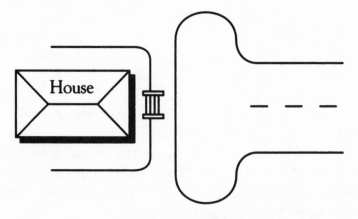

Figure 26: A house at the end of a cul-de-sac is in an inauspicious position. You should instigate a cure.

Cures for secret arrow energy are simple. Either place wind chimes in your porch (if you have one), plants either side of your doorway or, if you have the space, include a pond with a fountain. Use your own taste to decide. If you also incorporate one of the remedies from your own element you will begin to deflect the negative vibrations of secret arrow Ch'i. Your home and heart will then be off to a good start.

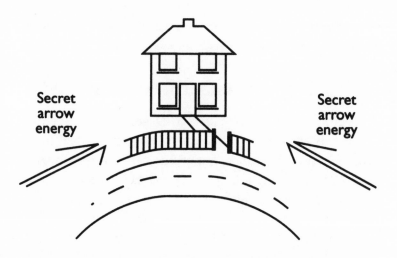

Secret arrow energy

Secret arrow energy

Figure 27: This house is vulnerable to secret arrow energy.

Is the garden in good shape? Is the front overgrown with weeds or strewn with rubbish? Does the path meander to the front door (if you have a path), or is it straight from the road and up the steps? Most people who live in urban environments will of course have straight paths or no paths at all. Rubbish and overgrown plants may be a reflection of your own inner state. If you always make excuses about clearing up the fallen leaves or the bits of paper flitting around the basement steps, maybe you're making excuses about your own life as well. Clearing up the rubbish and pruning the trees can have a remarkable effect on your relationships too!

If your home is at the end of a long straight path or up a steep rise of steps, a simple remedy like putting up hanging baskets or standing pots of winter pansies outside the door will deflect any difficult energy. If you live in a flat at the end of a long corridor, hang wind chimes outside your door, or next to the doormat place a tall terracotta pot containing a fallen tree branch.

Problem area: the kitchen

If the problem area of the Bagua corresponds to the kitchen, take a walk round it and check out a few facts. In traditional Feng Shui one of the most important things to remember is that Water and Fire are opposite energies. The first thing you should look at is whether the oven is next to the sink. Hot ovens = Fire; running taps = Water. Unfortunately, as most of us have fitted kitchens these days, there's not much you can do about separating Water and Fire in the kitchen if it's all built in and made to match.

If your oven and sink are close together, the remedy is to place a Wood cure either above or next to these intense energy sources to allow the energy to harmonize and thus prevent your problems from getting too hot! This could be something like a small plant on the shelf, a wooden spoon hanging on the wall between the oven and the sink, or maybe a photo of trees or a painting of the rainforests.

Kitchens are the most creative and energizing rooms in the house, according to Chinese philosophy. You may prefer the bathroom or the bedroom, but this is where life is energized; this is where food is cooked and the process of creating and blending ingredients is a magical and exciting experience. Most of us aren't quite so romantic about shoving the oven chips in the oven or the TV dinner in the microwave. But think about it. When you first fall in love, or develop a nesting instinct, what is it you most love to do (apart from falling into bed together, that is)? Cook a romantic dinner for two. If your kitchen is full of dirty dishes and stale food, old tins and out of date meals in the fridge, now is the time to do a bit of clutter removal. That romantic dinner for two won't ever get cooked by the soul and inner spirit if your heart and your home aren't ready for it. So if you're single and looking for love, look to your kitchen first and check out what is really on your menu tonight! If we keep our kitchens filled with good energy, our problem area may become less of a problem.

When you've cleared all the mess away and made sure the oven isn't clashing with the sink energy, there are several other important changes to make to ensure a healthy base for vitalizing harmony and dispelling those problems. Ovens should face the strongest source of natural light. In the northern hemisphere this will be to the south. (If you live south of the equator, it will be north.) If you can't afford to move your oven to the other end of the room, make sure you hang a mirror or crystal to reflect the natural light back to the oven. A White Quartz crystal is ideal for this, but if you choose a mirror use one with bevelled edges and a wooden frame.

After the bedroom, the kitchen is one of the most important places for the health of your relationships. You may like to incorporate your own element cure (see Chapter 5) in your kitchen once you have made the changes recommended above. Of course if your kitchen seems perfectly OK and the problem remains, place one of the lovestyle cures in this area as well.

Problem area: the bathroom or loo

Bathrooms are often a *big* source of trouble. It may not look like it, but the loo is the place where you can easily lose your man down the pan if you're not careful! Seriously, this is one room where you can't make major changes without calling in the plumber, so if you think your good energy is being flushed away with the remains of your nicely cooked romantic dinner, make positive additions to your bathroom wall instead.

First, ensure you always shut the loo lid after using it, and also the loo door. Don't put trailing plants on top of the cistern or on the floor below the level of the toilet. This attracts energy towards the downflow of the water.

If your problem area lurks in the bathroom, place candles around you when you bathe to create positive and vitalizing energy; burn sandalwood incense and ensure you have a single Rose Quartz crystal in the room – but don't put it on top of the cistern!

Problem area: the bedroom

When it comes to your sexual relationships, make sure you energize your bedroom. A glass or stone pyramid can be an excellent cure and vitalizer for a bedroom that represents problems. The power of the pyramid is that, even though it has sharp-faceted sides, it directs and attracts energy that may be flowing uneasily. First make sure that the room is uncluttered, that the bed does not point feet-first towards the door, and that there are no main beams above your head. (If there is a beam over your head, Chapter 13 explains the problem of energy hot spots and how to deal with them.) To cure your specific problem in the bedroom, hang wind chimes at the window and place an oval or round mirror to face the doorway and any other doorways that might be opposite your room.

Problem area: the living room

Apart from the kitchen, this room is the most important one when we socialize in the home. This is the room we invite outsiders into – friends, family, strangers. In a way it is our showpiece and a big mirror of who we are. After you've lived in a house or flat for a while, you get used to your surroundings and don't even notice the grubby fingermarks and coffee stains. But when you go to someone else's house your first impression remains with you for a long time, just like the first impression you have when falling in love, or when your eyes alight on a face across a crowded room. Impressions can be negative; we may feel uncomfortable with others' ideas and lifestyles. We all react in some way to others' surroundings, and we all reflect who we are in the public rooms of our own homes.

Try to take an objective look at your living room. A living room is exactly what it says it is – it lives and breathes you and your relationships. It is the threshold to your spirit! So if your problem area corresponds to the living room, try moving the sofa to face the window, and keep an empty space in the middle of the floor so that friends and strangers can move through this area without disrupting the energy flow that circles round the outside of the room.

Furniture here should have curved legs, arms and edges.

Place a mirror on the wall that reflects the most daylight, and choose colours that are welcoming and warm, such as soft terracottas, sage greens, apricots and ointment pink.

If your problem area falls in any other rooms that haven't been mentioned – a hallway, a landing, a staircase or a utility room – ensure the area is free from clutter and hang a White Quartz crystal in the most sunlit window or the area of strongest natural light. .

Chapter Twelve

Something Missing or Something Disturbing?

Something Missing in Your Love Life?

If you can't quite put your finger on why things may be going wrong for you, or there seems to be little chance of

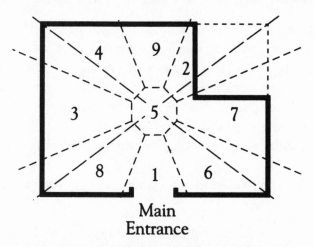

Main
Entrance

Figure 28: Missing Bagua. In this example a large
section of No. 2, Earth, is missing.

harmony for you in your relationships, it may be because, when you lay it over your home, part of the Bagua plan is literally missing.

Figure 28 shows a good example. Here the missing part of the Bagua is Earth. When this happens, whichever area it is you have missing, you must try to invite it back. Unusually shaped houses or those with extensions often have Bagua areas missing, and the remedy is to invite the energy back into your home with a simple mirror cure.

Place a mirror on the wall on the same side as the missing Bagua area; this creates the illusion that the room continues further than it actually does, and so invites the energy into that mirror space. Even if the missing Bagua area extends beyond a door or window, place a small convex mirror in the back of the door, or on the window ledge.

Something disturbing in your love life?

Another useful exercise is literally to put your feet up. Lie back in your favourite armchair, close your eyes and imagine yourself in each of the rooms of your house or home. If you live in a bedsit or share a house and have only one room to yourself, imagine yourself in different parts of the room. If you're trying to find out what is missing from your sexual relationship, imagine yourself on the bed in different positions.

Try to visualize the following images in each room or area of your home.

1 Does the room make you feel (a) comfortable or (b) uncomfortable?

2 Is it (a) warm and nourishing or (b) dark and menacing?

3 Do you (a) have a sense of freedom and purpose or (b) feel haunted by memories?

4 Do you feel (a) a sense of space or (b) one of claustrophobia?

5 Is there (a) peace and harmony or (b) too much noise – from external sources or within your head?

If you answer (b) to any of the questions, go straight to that room and begin removing the clutter and cleaning it up.

If you find any of the rooms stressful in any way as you are doing the visualization, make a mental note. Then place the Bagua over the plan of your home and find out which area of the Bagua and your relationship looks to be a source of disturbing energy. For example, you may have felt that your bedroom was a place haunted by memories. If you then place the Bagua over your home plan and find that Thunder corresponds to this room, all you have to do is use a Thunder cure to restore harmony.

Here are the Bagua remedies to place in a room or area that has disturbing energy.

If Water corresponds to the room – Fill a glass or stone cup with spring water. Sprinkle every evening with a little lavender scent or rosewater.

If Earth corresponds to the room – Place a piece of Malachite or Smoky Quartz on a window ledge or in direct sunlight.

If Thunder corresponds to the room – Find a piece of driftwood or a fallen branch and stand it beside the doorway.

If Wind corresponds to the room – Hang a small set of wind chimes in your window. Use ones that have a good musical quality.

If Core corresponds to the room – Place a piece of Rose Quartz in the centre of the room, or centrally on a table.

If Heaven corresponds to the room – Place a tall sculptural plant either in light or shade. Avoid cacti as their spiky quality produces discordant energy.

If Lake corresponds to the room – The simplest remedy is a single Bloodstone or, if that is unavailable, a red candle lit every evening.

If Mountain corresponds to the room – Hang a mirror facing your window to attract the qualities of both sunlight and moonlight.

If Fire corresponds to the room – Burn incense whenever you are in this room to cleanse and purify this powerful energy.

Chapter Thirteen

Powerful Energy Centres in Your Home

'There was a door to which I found no key: there was a
veil past which I could not see . . . '

This chapter tells you all you need to know about powerful
energy centres and how to deal with them. Remember how
beneficial energy moves in spirals and the negative energy –
secret arrow energy – moves in straight lines? With curves
we have gentle Yin, as the spiral keeps the energy in our
hearts; with fierce arrows of Yang energy we can lose love
and feel empty, as if the arrow has literally penetrated our
heart and gone out through the back of our bodies!

In your house there are certain places where powerful
energy centres can arise, both good and bad. If you aim to
nurture the good energies and allow space for the negative
energy to disperse, you will be able to keep a balance. This is
a reflection of what is going on in your heart and soul as
well. If you're keeping all that anger pent up and not letting
it out, it's going to work on you from the inside. Many

relationship problems are caused by an inability to express anger. But we all have anger and we must deal with it.

You may be a passionate sensual type who sometimes needs to throw a glass against the wall; just to make it difficult, your partner may be an airy intellectual who needs words and conversation to release aggression. Whatever your own methods of expressing your feelings, keeping a balance in the powerful energy spots in your home will help to channel this anger in the right way.

The energy spot that might give you most trouble or the greatest blessings is in the kitchen. This is because of the harmony achieved by preparing food, which is, of course a symbol of giving something good to ourselves, something to nourish and sustain us. The process of cooking reflects the blending of you and your partner, to see if you can transform the basic ingredients into something like well-risen wholemeal bread!

Energy in the kitchen

This is an important area for *sustaining* relationships. We've mentioned the cooker briefly in Chapter 11, but keeping a relationship alive and kicking could depend also on the way you keep your kitchen alive.

Fire illuminates and shows us the way forward. If you can cook, eat and be happy in your kitchen, you can love and transform your relationship too. The most important energy centre must be the cooker – electric oven, stove, Aga, two-ring camping gas or microwave. (However, it is strongly suggested that you don't just rely on a microwave. This is cold energy, not Fire but Metal. If you want a difficult relationship, living on microwave meals is a certain way to find one.)

The placement of stoves in Chinese houses was one of the intrinsic elements of good Feng Shui. Often practitioners would go straight to the stove and check out the location, the direction it faced and whether this was auspicious for the house and for the occupants.

Checklist

1 Is the cooker under a window? If yes, get it moved or the energy will disappear out of the window quicker than you can get the match relit. If you can't move it, hang some plants in the window, or put up a wooden rack and hang wooden spoons or spatulas to soak up the energy and re-direct it back into its kitchen spiral. (Wood is the element Fire needs to sustain it.)

2 Is the cooker directly opposite the back door? If yes, again you might need to move it. The Chinese sensibly always have their cookers placed so they can see the back door. This goes for any other items of furniture where you might be standing or sitting or lying. Never expose your vulnerable side to an open door. Turning your back on what may enter from behind is as dangerous as turning your back on someone you know is about to mug you. The secret arrows of dark and menacing Ch'i can stab you and your relationship in the back if you expose yourself to an open invitation.

3 Is the cooker facing enough light? Fire produces light, but most of our modern day cookers don't resemble a campfire or a bundle of sticks that shows up the food as it cooks. It is important to let natural light into your kitchen so that it falls across the food while it is cooking. If this is impossible,

hang a mirror to reflect the light down on to your food. (In the northern hemisphere this means the cooker should face south and a bit east; in the southern hemisphere it should face north and a bit east.)

Energy in the loo

This is an important place for defining our values, financial ones included, but more importantly those of desire.

The funny thing about the loo, whether it's a little room on its own or a loo in a bigger bathroom, is that the Chinese place great stress on making sure that the loo lid is always kept down. This is because, if you leave it open, rampant bad energy can take your pot of gold, or your ability to make a pot of gold may go down the pan with the rest of the waste matter.

Flushing away your fortune is a risky thing to do. But the kind of fortune symbolized here is the fortune we make in our relationships and who we attract by our desire. Every time you flush, remember to close the lid so your personal energy which enables you to desire and attract doesn't get drawn out into the sewers of the world!

Energy in the bed

This is an important centre for sexuality, transformation and psychic energy.

For obvious reasons, the bed is going to be a pretty potent place in any sexual relationship. But it is also the place where you sleep. Sleep is a wonderful thing if you aren't plagued by nightmares and terrible anxieties waking you up at 4 a.m. If your bed is placed in an awkward spot, you're going to have bad sex and bad sleep, so check it out.

Does the end of the bed point straight towards the doorway? If it does, try to move it or at least hang a mirror on the end of it to deflect any secret arrow energy coming straight at you.

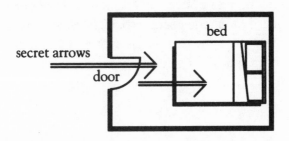

Figure 29: An inauspicious position for the bed.
Try to move it or hang a mirror on the end.

Many countries have superstitions about having your bed in such a position, mostly because when we're dead we are carried out feet first through the door. If your feet are pointing to the door when you're asleep, it won't make for a peaceful night. The secret arrows of malefic energy could also swoop in through the door and blaze their way straight across your bed. This could mean a broken relationship as well as broken sleep.

Are you lying directly under a main joist or heavy beam running perpendicular or horizontally over the bed? Either way, if the answer is yes, try to move the bed somewhere else. These kind of 'enemy lines' as I call them can destroy your sex life, your sleep and, most of all, your psychic energy. To get behind the enemy lines is, of course, one way of avoiding such conflict. If you can't move the bed or it ends up under another beam or joist, use some cunning and choose duvet covers (or sheets or blankets) that have strong lines in a pattern going at right angles to your beams. This will either take the enemy along the new lines and off the end of the bed, or deflect and balance the straight negative Ch'i.

Lastly, avoid lamps and lights hanging directly over your bed. This energy focuses strongly on whichever part of your body the light is hanging over and you may begin to suffer from aches and pains. Remove the lights immediately – or move the bed.

Chapter Fourteen

How to Deal with Inauspicious Energy

At some point in your life you will probably move house, either because you have to or because you want to. Remember that someone else may well have lived in your new home before you with all their baggage, emotional and otherwise. Coming upon all that energy left over from past occupants is a bit like moving into a house full of ghosts. If you feel you can't be comfortable in the kitchen because (a) it's a revolting shade of green and needs painting and (b) there's a definite air of coldness about the place, it may be that (b) needs just as much attention as (a). If we're in the middle of a good relationship, we may not be aware of the kind of energy that lingers on when people have left echoes of their own lives in the walls. The remedy is simple.

    1 Declutter and generally springclean the whole house or home.

    2 Bring in your favourite cure, one that is particularly suited to your element (or to both you and your partner).

    3 Use the lovestyle Bagua to decide which patterns of

energy are most important to you in your relationship now and implement the cures as described in Chapter 7.

4 Old 'heavy' energy from a bad marriage is easy to dispel. Light candles or incense and purify the room, break the old energy with a song, or, with open arms, literally sweep the energy from the room.

5 Once the old energy is gone, set yourself the task of welcoming yourself to your new home. Touch the walls, the furniture, the ceilings and the doors. Let the house know that you are there now, whether you are permanent or a temporary resident. This space is about interconnecting your energy and that of your friends and partners, not old worn-out energy that may have got left behind when past occupants moved away.

Finally, when you leave your old home make sure you take all your energy with you. It's simply a matter of pretending you are gathering the energy in your hands from each room as you leave. If the home is full of painful memories, take them with you but drop them outside in a space where they can disperse in the bigger energy fields and vibrations on the wind. Don't leave your bad energy for others. If it's sad to go, or the place has many good memories for you, then gather *them* up and take them with you. When you get to the new house, let them go carefully and place them in the Bagua area that feels most harmonious.

Now for the don'ts!

Here is an example of how *not* to use Feng Shui.

Jay and Susie had been involved in a relationship for five years, but neither wanted to move into the other's flat.

They both had successful careers and didn't want a conventional marriage or children – or at least, not yet.

Susie liked her independence and Jay was always charging off to Europe on business. However, Susie began to believe that Jay was 'looking elsewhere for sex' as she put it flippantly. He often forgot to phone her on his weekend trips abroad, and when he came over to her place he usually moaned about work, about travelling, and would rather put his feet up and watch TV than go to bed with Susie and a bottle of wine like in the old days.

'Our sex life is dead,' she confided on the phone one evening, so I suggested she instigate some subtle changes in the Lake area of her house and her bedroom. I suggested that she didn't insist on Jay using Feng Shui at least until things had begun to improve between them. But Susie was the kind of person who quite bluntly imposed her beliefs and opinions on her partner. She tried to coerce Jay into replanning his bathroom, hanging crystals in the window and generally doing up his bedroom the way she thought it should look, rather than in his own style. I believe she even sneaked round to his flat one day and did her own bit of curing! He was not amused. She came back to me a few days later with the grim news that Jay was off to Paris at the crack of dawn and had said it was about time they had a long break from each other.

But Susie persevered, decluttered her bedroom and, taking advantage of the fact that the Lake area of her flat was the kitchen, gave it a good springclean and then set to work with the remedies and cures I had originally suggested. Within a few weeks Jay had phoned Susie and agreed to talk about their relationship. They began to communicate more about their needs, and eventually Susie was able to suggest it might be a good idea if he moved his bed so it wasn't directly under a main beam.

The changes she had made on the outside were also beginning to work within. She had begun to perceive the dilemma of their relationship from a different perspective, which enabled her to listen to Jay rather than just assume she was right. And as she gradually began to look at who she was, and what it was that was bugging her about Jay, this in turn brought about a new respect for her own needs and Jay's needs. The energy rubbed off on Jay too. Ironically, Feng Shui worked for Susie, even though she could have blown the relationship to bits by her own presumptions.

Although things worked out for Susie eventually, the moral of the tale is don't blindly assume you have to change your partner's home too. Look to your own heart first!

Chapter Fifteen

The Remedies for Getting the Environment Right

This chapter gives a run-down of the remedies and cures that can be incorporated in your home. It's a useful sourcebook to look up extra ideas for your own element harmony, and how the actual remedies can add various energies to your environment. It also tells you how to use them successfully and how not to use them.

If you haven't yet read the chapters on lovestyles, elemental love and enhancement or done any of the exercises to find out what's going on in your home and in your heart, don't just turn to this chapter and start hanging mirrors and piling stones in heaps without exploring the rest of the book. Knowing what is going on within your love life is essential before you make any changes!

Colour

We all have our favourite colours, but your feeling about colour can change depending on your mood and situation.

175

Figure 30: Colour associations with the Bagua.

Red	Fire
Orange	Fire
Yellow	Earth
Ochre	Earth
Green	Thunder
Turquoise	Thunder
Blue	Water
Violet	Water
Purple	Lake
Black	Water
White	Heaven
Grey	Wind
Brown	Mountain

Reds

We associate this colour with Fire. Red is dynamic and exciting, and will stimulate and activate rather than mediate or moderate. In some cases reds and associated tones such as purple and pink can invigorate your sex life and add a dash of drama and anticipation to a romantic relationship – but handle with care. Don't use too much or you could cause destructive feelings to arise rather than merely dynamic ones.

In nature red is rare, so if you need loving tenderness and nurturing, you may find reds are too glaring and hot for any depth of intimacy to be achieved. Bring red into your life via small areas of concentrated passion rather than acres of wall space, unless you feel that the tremendous energy produced by such startling vibrancy will add that zest without love beginning to ferment.

In your bedroom, red or dusty pinks can be included in your bed decor, or in fabrics at windows. Red is also superb if you can find glass or china decorated with rich reds and oranges. A small keynote of red can enhance the kitchen – plastic kitchen utensils are often red. And for a reminder of how exotic and tempting your romantic liaisons can be, pick a red telephone. You may be amazed at how flirtatious and suggestive your communication becomes!

Blues

The blue spectrum can literally 'give you the blues' if you're not careful. Overloading your home with black and blue can make you depressed instead of allowing you to get in touch with your feelings so that you let them flow. Black can be incorporated via black and white photography or etchings, engravings and line drawings. Black jugs or dark blue china in the bathroom can do much to bring a sense of rhythm and flexibility into your love-nest. But if you indulge your hankering for deep blue in your overall colour scheme you may find yourself struggling with your inner world, dissolved by too many emotions and fears rather than aware of your needs and values. Blue and black undermine our sense of who we are if they are over-emphasized, whereas softer shades, a touch of charcoal black here and a hint of turquoise blue there, can augment and channel this valuable energy so that we don't lose touch with our egos but allow ourselves time to be who we really want to be.

Grey can be soothing and bring us a sense of purpose and give us time to reflect on what it is we want from our relationships. However, use it as if you were adding salt and pepper to a highly spiced curry; be cautious and blend it only in small amounts!

Greens

The energy here moderates our senses, and green can take us on a journey of realization, an upward spiral into a higher sense of self. Green traditionally allows us to get in touch with our roots, with nature, with the universe of which we are a part. Trees and plant life are valuable sources of green in our lives. In fact using natural greens, by bringing potted plants or even vegetables into your environment, is far more auspicious than painting your walls. But too much green can encourage daydreaming and romantic illusions. If you can see greenery from your home, either trees, parkland or someone's back garden, aim to make a feature of this view. However, delicate shades of green can be encouraged into your decoration with stencilled edges and borders or painted furniture. A highly auspicious use of green is on your front door. A green door allows us access to see out into the world as well as enabling us to welcome the energy of natural freedom within our lives.

Yellows

This includes all the earthy shades such as chestnut, brown and honey. Natural materials like hessian and jute can play a big part in extending the range of this colour in our homes. Sunshine yellow works wonders in a kitchen but do we really want it producing such stimulating energy in our bedrooms? Yellow is about inspiration and beliefs; it can remind us of our desires and energize our sense of reality. Grounding our senses is sometimes necessary to confront the truth of any relationship. Yellow ochre is a colour which can give us a sense of serenity and yet also remind us how jealous we can be at times. The irony of yellow is that it nurtures us as well as makes us hunger for more! Spring flowers are often yellow, but instead of plonking a bunch of daffodils in a vase at Easter, try finding yellow flowers in November and using them skilfully in some abstract form.

White/silver

The use of whites and silvers in your home can greatly enhance your self-esteem and determination to succeed in any relationship. White walls are a common feature of many homes and can be practical and enhancing in their own right. However, too much white can lose a relationship. It can become cold and critical, sharply defined, with no room to move. White is abstract because it is a balance of all the vibrations of the other colour energies. It can bring purity and integrity if used subtly throughout your home but, if over-emphasized, loneliness and melancholy are the result.

Whites can be incorporated easily into any environment, but silver is a more powerful aspect of white which stirs eroticism in any kitchen, bedroom or loo! By the way, silver is the only element that can destroy a werewolf. In ancient Chinese folklore there was a tale about a wolf-child that ate out the hearts of those it loved because it could never grow old. Maturity is silver and it was with a rod of silver that a wise old mystic stabbed the child-wolf who was then transformed into a silver dragon. Of course, the silver dragon brings you much success and happiness, so using silver in your home can increase your chances of success in any relationship.

Mirrors

The person with whom you share your life or with whom you are romantically involved is in fact a reflection of you. In a way, as you gaze lovingly into your partner's eyes you are looking into a mirror. What you love, need and desire in a partner are in fact those qualities that are deeply buried in you, that you may not be aware of, but find so enticing in someone else. This is called projection. Projection can also include a lot of negativity; people who always end up with vindictive partners are often unconsciously attracted to these types because they aren't aware of what is going on in their own unconscious. If you have mirrors in your home that reflect the energy you create, make sure you are putting out good or auspicious energy in the first place.

Mirrors should always be kept as clean and lovingly polished as possible. Avoid cracked mirrors. Remember the lines from Tennyson:

> *The mirror crack'd from side to side;*
> *'The curse is come upon me,' cried*
> *The Lady of Shalott.*

If for any reason your mirrors are cracked or scratched, get rid of them.

Use big mirrors rather than tiny ones which reflect only a small part of you. The bigger the mirror the more energy it is reflecting, and the more you may find the vibrancy and dynamics of your relationship come to life. Make sure mirrors are not reflecting ugly spots, like cluttered bookshelves, the dirty laundry basket, the dustbin, a blank wall, the loo or electrical cables and points. The electricity in a room is highly charged energy, and there's enough in anyone's home as it is without doubling the vibrations with badly angled or misplaced mirrors.

Try to use curved mirrors rather than square or oblong ones. If you have no choice, make sure you have an element of Water near to hand, to help the energy flow.

Don't sleep directly in front of or below a mirror (unless you are part of an Earth combination, in which case you probably have enough energy to balance this out). A mirror by the bed may enhance your sexual dynamics but make sure that once the fun is over and you're resting, you are not actually reflected in the mirror. This energy is too active and you may find you don't get much sleep. Fine if you're having a steamy night, but disastrous if you need to be up early in the morning.

Using mirrors as a remedy

If you have a strange shaped home or room like the one in Figure 31, you may have part of your Bagua missing. In this case mirrors are excellent for creating the illusion that this area exists in your home. Although it is only an illusion, the reflection brings the missing Bagua area to life. In a sense you are projecting that part of the Bagua in rather the same way that you project yourself into your relationships.

In this example, the missing area of the Bagua is Thunder. By placing mirrors on the walls (as shown in the diagram) you can 'create' that missing area. Mirrors let energy flow, so they both enable you to create Thunder and restore the energy balance.

Most of the mirrors used in the East are in the form of an octagon like the shape of the Bagua. This reflects all the spirals of energy and, if placed at the end of a long hallway

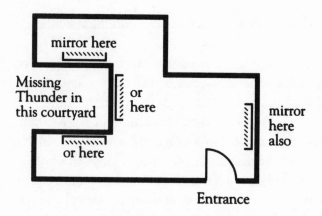

Figure 31: Using mirror placements to bring missing Bagua area to life.

or at the back door, enables auspicious energy to stay in the home, while deflecting bad or stagnant energy out of your environment.

As we've already seen, mirrors can enhance the elemental balance of missing Fire in your relationships. But mirrors, like colours, should be used with discretion. Use a small octagonal mirror in your bathroom or bedroom to deflect difficult energy; this adds flavour to colour and light effects and stirs physical and potent sexual energy. But don't think that you have to change your style to incorporate mirrors if you don't actually like them. Be inventive and add a mirror image or even dramatize one existing mirror that means something to you. Even if you just surround it with a new frame or paint the edging gold, you will have put *you* into the reflective quality as well as into your relationship – which is, after all, a reflection of you.

Wind chimes

The ubiquitous wind chimes are now so much part of our everyday life that we may have begun to lose the essence of what their music means. For the Chinese they are an essential component for good energy, good vibrations and harmony. They are the music that brings a subtle shift or emphasis to the energy flow of your home. As they are used particularly for those who are lacking the element Wood in their environment, they convey not only a more aesthetic quality to a relationship but also greater responsiveness and co-operation with others.

When you buy wind chimes, go for the ones that really sing to you. Their tonal qualities vary, so make sure you are in tune with the vibration and the music before you start hanging them in your Bagua areas. (Some people buy any old wind chimes, hang them in their windows or near open doors and think they're going to transform their lives.) You should use wind chimes where you want to moderate the energy that enters or leaves your home, rather than trapping it or redirecting it.

If you hang your wind chimes in windows, you may find that you never hear them except in summer when the windows are open. Avoid hanging them where you won't get a flow of energy. Near front and back doors, in hallways and porches or even in open carports or on sheltered terraces or patios are all good places. As long as you like the sound and the wind chimes don't turn into a clattering mas of metal clinks every time the wind blows, you will hav achieved the essence of your music. Avoid having too man different tonal qualities of wind chimes competing again one another for the best sound. This may not only be discordant to the vibrations of the natural energy but also set up conflict and ambivalence in your love life instead of development and progress.

Water

If you don't live beside a natural pond or lake, or by a running brook or a wide expanse of river or the sea, you may need to bring water into your home by other means. Water helps relationships to flow, so equally it's important not to invite stagnant areas of water into your home. You may think you're bringing in the goldfish bowl to add sensitivity to your Mountain Bagua area, when in fact the water never gets changed and clouds up with fishy excrement. Would you like your relationship to reflect this mess? If an aquarium seems an ideal solution, ensure you add a filter to keep the water crystal clear and flowing.

A jug of coloured water can be a wonderful addition to a bedroom or bathroom windowsill, but again, change it frequently or you will end up with stagnant smelly water. If you are feeling incredibly wealthy, a waterbed or even an indoor fountain could emphasize good communication and the ability to be flexible. Paintings depicting the sea or waterfalls can be used instead of the real thing if you're not lucky enough to be able to indulge in a jacuzzi or a spa bath, but make sure you have at least one shower unit, even if it's simply a rubber attachment. Just turning the water on and letting it flow can help you in times when you need to be more adaptable in your relationships.

Light

Some of us hate bright lights and prefer the dim glow of side lamps and candles. Others can't stand candles and want sharply focused Anglepoise lights to see their way clearly. Whatever your choice, remember that light brings optimism and daring into your love life, and smoochy candlelight signals romance, provocation and fantasy! If you want to accentuate a painting or a special corner of your room, use uplighting as well as downlighting.

Whatever makes you feel comfortable can enhance the area of the Bagua that may be missing in your own love life by focusing the light source on to that spot. Bold light brings dramatic energy to a bedroom, but it may result in cold emotions. Soft and subdued lights will make the room spin with eroticism and/or serenity. Light is an active principle in Feng Shui. Candlelight fills a space with enough energy to incite dynamic sex.

Bright spots

Sparkling objects such as crystals, gemstones, beads and shiny metallics can, if need be, augment the sense of light. Hanging polished crystals in your window does wonders for this kind of energy and the facets of cut glass or prisms are extraordinary ways of taking light and scattering it about your room like a million rainbows. If you're lucky enough to have stained glass windows in your house, take advantage of their powerful activating energy. If you don't have any, you may be able to find an old piece of stained glass in a second-hand shop or junk yard that you can place in front of an existing window to energize the Ch'i. New stained glass, by the way, is not so auspicious as the colours are not as pure as the colours that were used in pre-war glass windows. However, if you can't get hold of any old leaded stained glass, make sure you find modern pieces that have good hues and tones, subtle rather than stark.

Flora

Plants are one of the easiest ways to add a touch of the Wood element to your Bagua, and probably the simplest way to direct beneficial energy into your life. However, some plants can have negative results so it's worth making a note of the ones that you may have trouble connecting to your environment.

Ivies and anything that trails can turn your well-meaning seduction into a depressing dream.

Speckled plants may create dissension between partners.

Upright plants need lots of space or they can fill the atmosphere with compulsive arrogance.

Avoid dried flowers, except in the winter.

Try to use flowers that are seasonal.

Potted plants that come from jungles and rainforests should be used only if you are a Water element character.

Use plants with soft and rounded leaves. The Ch'i is more harmonious. Spiky plants invite conflict.

Lastly, choose plants that don't take over the home. Their invasion of your energy can cause a disturbance in the Bagua.

Fauna

Pets are great if you really care for them and love them. If you decide to invest in a tropical fish tank or goldfish aquarium, treat the fish as you would your best friend! Dogs and cats are highly sensitive to their environment, so watch them carefully if you make any dramatic changes around the home. You may find they instinctively congregate round good energy spots and avoid the unpleasant ones.

Crystals

Crystals have been known for their power to charge up energy and have been used as a healing tool for centuries. If you don't yet know much about crystals, it's worth discovering which ones suit your temperament and your relationship so that you can wear them as well as place them in the home. When you choose a crystal, allow yourself to be drawn to one that stands out for you. This intuitive process reflects your ability to know yourself and trust your instincts. Natural rock crystals are part of Earth energy, and can be highly grounding and healing.

The placement of crystals is important but, if you prefer, you can carry them round in a pouch or as jewellery.

If you have a chance, take your new crystal down to the seaside and wash it in sea water. This sets the vibrational energy in balance. If you can't get to the sea, wash it in mineral water but don't add salt. Natural brine is very different from salty tap water!

Art

This is a matter of personal choice. If you are fascinated by watercolours, addicted to abstract prints, or totally hate anything on your walls except photos of your family, keep to your own rules and don't try to change for the sake of it. Adapt your original choices either by adding beneficial elements or by taking away obvious trouble-makers from the Bagua areas that are in need of change.

For example, don't throw out the abstract prints that you've had hanging in the loo but move them to a more auspicious part of the house. Abstract paintings have a Fire quality and you may be placing too much emphasis on a dynamic relationship which can't function if it's in the Wind area (the loo) of your Bagua.

Form

This includes things like pebbles, fossils, shells, natural objects and wood, furniture and sculpture. The outside world can be brought into your inner world through many things. Our gardens, paths, terraces and communal hallways are also part of our wider living Bagua, so it might be advisable to look at these outer areas in your life. This is where form can help, because it's not always easy to place a candle in the communal hallway of a block of flats, if you find this to be the missing area of your Bagua. However, a fairly unobtrusive stone at the top of a stairwell or beside your entrance door may be enough to balance and restore harmony.

Chapter Sixteen

The Five Elemental Energies and You

Chinese astrology gives us great insight into the kind of energy we project and attract, whether it is through our relationships or in the way we express ourselves in our homes. Most people have come across the twelve Chinese animal signs; Rat, Ox, Tiger, Rabbit, Dragon, Snake, Horse, Sheep, Monkey, Rooster, Dog and Boar.

Fewer people in the West are familiar with the five elements that form an integral guide to your own energy awareness. The five elements of energy are used extensively by Feng Shui practitioners not only to work out your birth chart but also to create a similar chart for your house and even the site it is built on. This ancient system of growth and change is reflected in every area of the Bagua and you.

As you now know, the five elements represent the five different forces of energy, the kinds of Ch'i that are manifested in the world, whether through our bodies, nature, colour, smells or simply through love. Chinese astrology is based on a system of creation and destruction. Figure 32 explains how this works.

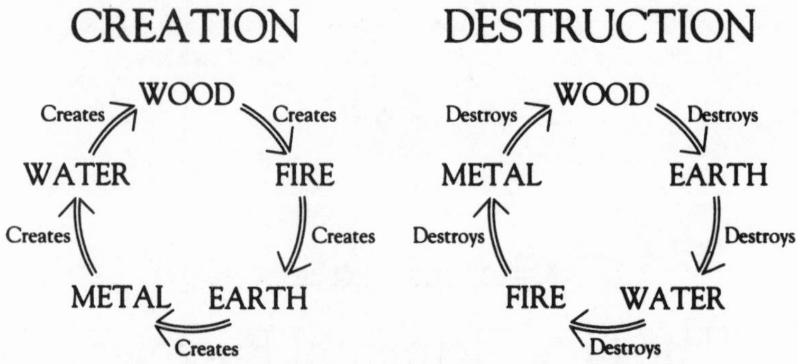

CREATION   DESTRUCTION

Figure 32: Cycle of creation and destruction.

The Bagua is part of this system and the Feng Shui compass in Figure 33 shows you how all these elements, compass directions and animal signs interrelate to form a never-ending cycle.

Tips for balancing elements

1 The five elements form a cycle of energy that must be balanced and harmonized in your own environment depending on which element you are. For example, if you are a Fire elemental lover, you may need to express this side of yourself in your surroundings, but you will also need to draw on the other elements which complement Fire, i.e. Wood and Earth. If your partner lives in the same home and he/she is Water, he/she may need Water in some form, but also Metal and Wood to complement and enhance the harmony.

2 The best tip to remember is that whatever element you are, expressing this side of yourself is the key to using and nourishing it. To bring harmony into your love life use your own element cures, but don't overload the home! To

balance this energy so that it works positively for you, you may need to enhance your environment with other complementary elements.

Here are the complementary elements:

Fire can benefit from Wood and Earth cures
Earth can benefit from Metal and Fire cures
Metal can benefit from Water and Earth cures
Water can benefit from Wood and Metal cures
Wood can benefit from Fire and Water cures

**Figure 33: Simple version of the
Feng Shui compass.**

The elements in our environment

Wood

The associations for Wood are fairly obvious. Don't imagine just because wood is solid and rooted that this energy is static. It's highly potent which is unsurprising when you realize how long it takes for a tree to grow and how much energy is required. The tree has grown because it has been nourished with Water. (In the cycle Water creates Wood.) Wood energy is magical and that's why trees have been used as symbols for growth and fertility in many different cultures for centuries. Creativity is symbolized by upward movement that takes us beyond the ground, beyond reality as we know it. Even though we are rooted to the earth we can climb towards the sky.

Trees are essential in the Wood energy cycle for even if they have been chopped down or uprooted by storms they still serve a purpose. We are surrounded by wooden objects, from furniture and books to the flowers, plants and trees in our garden, or the ones we import into our home. Wood is associated with the colour green, and all natural plant life. If, for example, you find that this element needs to be harmonized in both your home and heart, even by adding something as simple as cushions or fabrics that have used vegetable dyes rather than chemical ones, you'll already have taken the first step.

In traditional Feng Shui, Wood is also associated with green dragons, the spring and the direction east.

Fire

Fire is about action. It ascends and burns, it gives us light and awareness. The problem with Fire is that too much of it can scorch us. Wood enables us to light a fire and to keep it fuelled and active. (Wood creates Fire in the cycle.) Although Fire is a stimulating element, it can lead to flames that move too fast, like the forest fire that rages out of control and destroys all in its path.

But Fire is also warmth, sunlight and passion. It has long been associated with the sun and the summer. Red and orange are Fire colours, as is anything shiny or bright. Red is not a colour often seen in the natural world so it may be difficult to bring it into your house without resorting to paints, coloured fabrics or artwork.

Too much red can be overpowering. Although it's a great colour in a bedroom to enhance passion and eroticism, it must be carefully blended in the rest of the home. You could include red cabbage in your kitchen, red candles in the living room or red light bulbs in your bathroom! Fire in traditional Feng Shui is symbolized by the phoenix and the direction south. It is very Yang (masculine) energy and because it looks only to the future, rather than the past or the present, it must be used with care.

Earth

You're left with ashes after the Fire has burnt away the heart of the Wood, and Earth is the result. Earth energy is simple energy. It is associated with any object that comes from the ground (apart from precious metal), so stones, pebbles, crystals and rock can be included for harmonious Earth environments. The Earth is the nourisher of all things, and is concerned with our seasons, our inventions of time and matter, and our sense of purpose. Earth is about the here and now and the boundaries we create for ourselves and for others. Earth wants to make useful the abstract, and to manifest ideas and feelings on the material plane. It's also about nature, and about physical reality. Other associations of Earth are tranquillity and peace, because Earth avoids conflict however hard Fire would like to instigate it!

Both the north-east and the south-west are symbolized by Earth. Earth energy is ancient although it carries the past forward, it also brings the present into focus. Yellow is Earth's colour, and in the home yellow can soothe and inspire. Brown may also be included, although it may be a difficult colour to use in your decor. Think of brown stones and ochre walls. Soft terracotta colours, shades of rocks, natural sand and neutrals can be included in the Earth range. Earth is also symbolic of early autumn, of harvest and the changes of the bright summer light to softer rays as the equinox approaches.

Metal

The Chinese are fond of the energy of this element when Metal is put to its most positive use, which is, of course, making money. Metal's goal is prosperity. But Metal is also about communication, the west and north-west.

Gold is highly significant for Metal energy and you often find gold leaf, gold paint, gold everything in the Chinese home. However, when in Rome . . . Remember that little saying? What may seem right in a Chinese or Eastern culture, where the climate, the smells and the light are different, can look distinctly out of place in a town flat or suburban house in the West. Don't overload your home and body with gold ornaments which don't fit in with your lifestyle. It just won't work. The art of Feng Shui is to use the symbols of the energies in a way which is suited to your society and your lifestyle, interior design and choices. Changing your house to look like an ancient Chinese palace won't be the answer to your problems, and may give rise to some strange questions from your friends and relatives, bringing more Thunder into your home than you bargained for!

This energy has traditional associations with anything Metal, whether it is gold, silver, stainless steel or wrought iron. It represents white and the end of autumn, when the weather is turning colder and drier. Earth solidifies over time to become Metal, and what Earth has found in the real world can now be put into words and abstracted by Metal. That is why Metal both carries and symbolizes the power of knowledge. White signifies the purity of no-colour. Any Metal, whether in the form of gold, silver, steel, cars, aeroplanes, cookers, fire grates, metal furniture – these are all excellent Metal element enhancers or cures. Metal energy is associated with transformation, justice and moving forward both financially and spiritually.

Water

The motion and the stillness of Water can be either stirring or stagnating. Water is always fluid and is symbolic of energy that is reflective and instinctive. Water is involved with the origins of things, whether of our feelings, emotions or life itself. Water is about infinity and about symbols which themselves mirror our feelings. Water is concerned with the magical and the practical but more importantly it represents that shadow of ourselves beyond the unconscious, the part of ourselves that stays hidden.

Water is easily brought into our homes in different ways – with a fish tank, a tiny stone cup filled with sea water or an outrageous waterbed! Just by enabling Water to be expressed in your daily routine through bathing, showering or drinking mineral water, you will enhance this element if it is lacking in your life. Traditionally Water corresponds to the colours blue and black. Fountains, rivers, waterfalls and aquaria have always been used for Feng Shui enhancement wherever possible, together with objects that stimulate the flow of water, such as an image of high cliffs in a painting or photo. Water also symbolizes winter, the north and cold rainy weather. In our Western society blue is rarely used in a north-facing room because it appears to make the room darker and more depressing, but sometimes blue can work extremely well in a north-facing environment to deepen and add mystery to an otherwise cold and forbidding light. Both blue and black should be used with care in Feng Shui enhancement. Black, particularly, draws in all colours of the spectrum, and with it your psychic energy.

Checklist of element cures

Wood: Furniture, chairs, cupboards, books, plants, sculpture, green, vegetable dyes, east, green dragons, herbs, sage, rosemary, thyme, mint, forest green, soft twilight hues, spring meadows, high corn, olive green, gnarled wood, wooden sculpture, wood fires, oil paints, spreading plants, grasses, dried seed pods, origami, ladders, staircases, steps.

Fire: Sun, summer, red/orange, brightness, lighting, red cabbage, red light bulbs, the phoenix, south, mirrors, candles, incense, real fires, crystals, reflectors, prisms, drama, mythology, fantasy, bells, spices, cacti, rubber plants, gloss paint, Indian red, smoking jacket crimson, highly strung colours, firework paintings, stars, battleships, bonfires, red glass.

Earth: Stones, pebbles, rocks, rock crystal, yellow, brown, ochre, north-east, south-west, terracotta, dusky desert yellows, antiques, shells, fossils, loofahs, sponges, glass jars, drab greens, honeycombs, eggshell finishes, soaps, scents, essences, tapestries, old fabrics, paisleys, Japanese landscapes, bonsai trees, rich umber, burnt sienna, coffee and tea.

Water: Fish tanks, stone cups filled with water, sea water, waterbed, bathing, drinking, blue/black, fountains, objects that stimulate the flow of water, winter, north, watercolours, music, rivers, stones and rocks from the sea, soft sheen water-based paints, violet, viridians, Prussian blue, sea paintings, pirates, wrecks, ships, boats, cliffs and waves, lakes, icebergs, amber, coloured inks.

Metal: Gold leaf, silver, stainless steel, wrought iron, white, cars, cookers, stoves, ovens, fire-grates, metal furniture, west, north-west, photography, line drawings, etchings, engravings, kitchen utensils, scrap metal, gilt picture frames, jewellery, mock gold, brilliant white, bedsteads, brass rubbings, Tantra, silver threads, gold-coloured fabrics, white lilies, stars.

Elemental phases

Before you read the section for your birth element take a look at the checklist below because you may be going through a different element energy phase from the one under which you were born.

Read each checklist and see which elemental personality style seems to match up with you. It is quite natural to feel and to activate elements other than the one we were born under when we pass through different stages in our lives. Don't worry, for example, if you feel distinctly unlike a Metal person even though that is your designated birth element, and feel more in touch with, say, Water energy. It is advisable to read both sections and link them up, because although you may be going through a stage or cycle the underlying energy of your birth element remains highly significant. You may be going through a phase where, for example, you are expressing more Fire than your birth element Water would lead you to expect. As already discussed, we are made up of all the elements and must travel along all their roads at some point in our lives, so follow the journey you feel is relevant to you right now.

If you were born either on the very last day of an elemental cycle or the very first day of a new one, it might be advisable to look at both elements, as the actual times of these lunar cycle changes aren't given. You may feel that one element is more you than the other.

Your birth element

Energy changes, and although your dominant element may not be the one you were born under, the birth element is still a good guide to the cycle of energy which will emphasize your expressions in love and life. Don't take it as absolute that if you were born under Fire you have to behave like a Fire person! But remember the underlying energy is there, so adapt to it, and blend it into your harmonious living and loving.

Overview

The elemental guide can give you some idea as to how you express your elemental energy. If you use this information in conjunction with the cures and remedies for creating harmony in your home, you will get an overview of your whole way of relating and the way others relate to you. Remember, what you put into your environment is a reflection of what you put into your relationships. The spirals of energy are there in your heart as well as your home.

Yin and Yang

At the end of each element section is a guide to sexual expression, whether you are born under a Yin year or a Yang year.

If you were born under a Yin year, you are more inclined towards expressing Yin energy. This is passive, receptive and flowing energy.

If you were born under a Yang year, you are more inclined towards expressing Yang energy. This is active, dynamic and potent energy.

Birth element checklist

Read the following checklist for your birth element first, before looking at the detailed sections on your love expression.

1 You may find that the element you were born under doesn't describe you at the moment. But if you can tick off

at least 15 of the 27 identity expressions listed, then read your birth element.

2 However, if you feel that another element sums you up in your current situation, read that one too. You may also travel through another elemental stage in your life and be able to connect to one of the other elements more directly than your given birth one. In this case, again, if you can tick off at least half of the expressions given, refer to that element as if it were your own.

FIRE

Impulsive	Passionate	Dynamic
Dominating	Proud	Tactless
Optimist	Self-centred	Active
Daring	Romantic	Intuitive
Independent	Audacious	Impatient
Demanding	Childlike	Exuberant
Fun-lover	Risk-taker	Pushy
Provocative	Fantasizer	Headstrong
Inciting	Urgent	Vain

EARTH

Sensual	Affectionate	Patient
Possessive	Self-aware	Pragmatic
Cautious	Stubborn	Receptive
Emotional	Tenacious	Lustful
Seductive	Jealous	Serene
Aloof	Sexual	Materialist
Artistic	Introspective	Capable
Consistent	Acquisitive	Nurturing
Nature-loving	Persistent	Indulgent

METAL

Powerful	Erotic	Intense
Single-minded	Autonomous	Inflexible
Torrid	Secretive	Arrogant
Extremist	Lonely	Instigator
Compulsive	Melancholic	Ambitious
Determined	Dedicated	Highly sexed
Realistic	Successful	Magnetic
Regenerative	Distinctive	Astute
Integrity	Sagacious	Cynical

WOOD

Altruistic	Sophisticated	Detached
Perfectionist	Cool	Diplomatic
Ambivalent	Freedom-loving	Experimental
Broad-minded	Opinionated	Co-operation
Egotistic	Eccentric	Poised
Liberal	Idealist	Alluring
Seductive	Responsive	Sociable
Extrovert	Humanitarian	Scattered
Aesthetic	Fears intimacy	Unpossessive

WATER

Communicative	Romantic	Elusive
Flexible	Sensitive	Gullible
Passive	Airy	Unfocused
Fickle	Unpredictable	Witty
Inconsistent	Changeable	Neurotic
Intuitive	Noncommittal	Escapist
Imaginative	Gregarious	Beguiling
Persuasive	Charming	Clever
Fluid	Transient	Impressionable

Compatible and Incompatible elements

The most difficult element with which Fire can merge, whether in the home or as a partner, is Water. Fire and Water are natural polarities in Feng Shui and in the natural world. Water people can neutralize and sometimes blow out Fire's passion and desire for life and love. However, Fire is often attracted to Water types, simply because they appear to be so different!

We all have a blend of the elements within us, and if Fire can learn to live with Water's ebb and flow, their currents of feeling and sensitivity, and their longing to find something beyond fantasy and reality, Fire may discover something about him/herself. This same premise goes for Wood and Metal, and Earth and Water as well. If you look at the compatibility chart below you'll see which elements are comfortable and naturally harmonious, and which are out of balance to your own.

Compatibility chart: harmony and disharmony.

Element	Harmonious	Niggly	Uncomfortable
Wood	Fire and Water	Earth	Metal
Fire	Wood and Earth	Metal	Water
Earth	Metal and Fire	Water	Wood
Metal	Water and Earth	Wood	Fire
Water	Wood and Metal	Fire	Earth

Elements of the same type, such as Wood and Wood, have an innate empathy.

Take the above example: if you are Fire in a relationship with Water, by balancing other elements in your environment you may well find that Fire and Water prove to be a perfect union of opposites. No one is all Fire and no one is all Water, so remember that however Fire or however Water you may feel, there is a locker-room in your personality that contains the other hidden elements.

Now move on to the next chapter and read your element personality type. This may help you to understand the kind of relationships you need, and also be a trigger for harmonious energy to enter your life.

Chapter Seventeen

Love Expressions

Fire man

'Don't play with fire.'

Burning yourself, either on a real fire or on the embers of someone with the passion and impulses of Fire, can be a pretty painful way to learn about life. Yet if you are a Fire element type then this may seem like nonsense! Fire males need adventure, excitement and risk-taking. They also need relationships, and lots of them. This doesn't mean Fire is promiscuous, but many a Fire subject can burn his way through another's heart if he is feeling impatient and passionate about life. Passion is an important word to the Fire type. He has an inner need to look forward to the next event, sometimes to the next lover, especially if the one he is with can't keep up with his enthusiasm and zest for life. Highly motivated to rage his way through life's landscape, Fire may at times seem unstoppable. But even the Fire man needs to find a balance in life so that he doesn't burn himself out. Fire is about inspiration and the future. To Fire the past is someone else's book, an old film or video that is long past rewinding. It may just be that because of Fire's need to get on with life and never stop, he will reach more people and experience more pleasure and pain than any other element. A good deal of luck seems to appear on his doorstep and he can take advantage of it in a flash. Fire needs to express his ardour at times, so fiercely and quickly that he gets caught up in more escapades and entanglements than he had ever bargained for.

In love Fire can be at fault. He tends to be irresponsible about commitment, refusing to listen to others' needs and often so wrapped up in himself that he doesn't have time to consider anyone else's viewpoint. What you have to remember most about Fire is that he loves to play – which is why the phrase 'don't play with fire' is so ideally suited to him. He needs to play with life. A bit like Prometheus who stole Fire from the Gods and gave it to humanity, the Fire male has a habit of playing with anything dangerous and enjoying the risk more than the actual outcome. The Fire man is a doer. The end result is irrelevant, he just goes ahead and does it, whatever it is. Once a game ends he moves on to the next one, and the next risk.

Fire is a kid at heart, and fantasizes about love and relationships. This is why he falls in love and enjoys romance so easily, but when reality arrives in the guise of commitment, paperwork, practicalities and routine in his love life, he either skids off round the block in his fast car or falls in love with someone else.

Sex is not just a physical act to a Fire element male, it symbolizes the whole of his way of being. The trouble with expressing his sometimes unusual desires is that his partner may find it difficult to understand why Fire often prefers romantic and erotic fantasies to the sexual act itself. An extreme Fire element type may be attracted to strongly Earth element types. This is a common projection of Fire's lost Earth element that gets demoted behind the dreams. Earth expects a lot more sexual intercourse and sensual experiences than Fire can come up with, and this can push Fire into feeling as though he is expected to perform for the sake of it! At this point the end of the relationship often seems in sight. Reality is something that Fire males would rather avoid. If they can't stay in their dreams and schemes, they'd rather get out and run.

Fire is more inclined to sudden physical outbursts of passion than any other element. This is the passion of Eros (not the Cupid image we all associate with Valentine cards but Eros as a concept of erotic and passionate love); without any other kind of love to stabilize him, the Fire hothead can often burn out his own desire and wonder why the woman he is with is no more exciting than any of the others he knew before. That's why, in Feng Shui, it can be crucial to balance very Fiery types with both Earth and Wood remedies.

Desire is a word close to the Fire male's heart. But it is a desire for ideal love itself rather than for an individual. He projects this desire on to many that he meets. Physical attraction is the Fire element's hook, and yet once sure of his soul-mate, he is loyal and attuned to her needs. He is honest and bold, sometimes tactlessly so when he admits he could love many women. Other men hate him and most women adore him.

Getting involved with a Fire type is dangerous, unless you are prepared to take the risk he longs to take. Fire needs to feel free and easy. He avoids emotional hang-ups and can't bear possessive company. However, Fire men can be acutely jealous if their current flame starts to blow towards another stack of twigs!

What Fire needs to express are his love of living, his love of romance and passion and his need to play games. In a relationship that is free and yet loyal, that is not hemmed in by emotional boundaries or overloaded with emotional blackmail, he will enjoy himself and perhaps be less likely to seek his ideal outside such a partnership. The problem for Fire is that he needs to get in touch with his senses and with the world, for often he has great trouble staying in contact with reality. He doesn't want a mother, he wants a lover, but one who won't make him feel he has to be making love to her all night. For the Fire man's soul needs to be turned on more than his loins. He needs the stories in his head and the messages in his spirit first, and then perhaps he may begin to enjoy the close contact and sensuality of a transforming relationship.

Fire woman

'Long misled by wandering Fires . . . '

Fire has a habit of taking hold in the wrong place when the wind blows too hard. Similarly, the Fire woman will impulsively leap into the arms of the wrong guy. The problem for a Fire woman is that her ideals are big and her love is infectious, and if a relationship looks like the answer to her dreams she doesn't stop to ask questions first. Romance never dies for a Fire woman. Fire needs to play at her speed and often at her instigation; for if she's not afraid of picking up a man, she's certainly not afraid of dropping him either! The Fire lady needs to envelop and promote, to activate and desire, and with the blind and often irrational impulses of the child she really is, this woman will sweep men off their feet and probably irritate a few other ladies into the bargain.

Most Fire women want to be in charge in the relationship. Because they are usually good-looking and need exclusive attention, they often attract the kind of men who can easily be swamped by such an independent style of love. The Fire woman may enjoy this for a while and, just like the Fire male, she will play many games with those fair-skinned types who burn too easily. Playing the lead role is the most important thing in a Fire woman's life and, if she doesn't get her way, the relationship will fall apart just as quickly as it began. A Fire woman knows intuitively what she wants, and she usually gets it. Like her male equivalent, she has enough sexual magnetism and charm to get away with murder.

But Fire needs friendship too. Sex is one thing, a game and an amusement, but friendship and companionship are the most enduring qualities in any Fire woman's eyes. The difficulty is that, like male Fire types, she needs to satisfy her own needs first and her partner's either this year, next year or sometime never! She often has an unrealistic view of what a relationship is, and may assume that her partner should do all the work, whether sexually to keep her aroused or mentally to keep her mind alert. She has high expectations of sexuality and is motivated to be there for that other person if her loyalty is returned and her integrity upheld.

There is more optimism, hope and desire in a Fire woman's heart than in any other element, and her honesty and sensitivity – yes, there really is a great sensitive heart down there underneath the brash glowing flame of passion – may take a while to seep through her preoccupation with self-image and self-love. But once anyone gets there, she is probably one of the better elements for making others happy because she needs to feel so happy herself.

The Fire woman can teach by *being* what she expects from others. In other words, she needs to be fulfilled, needs to be free, to be spirited and the centre of attention. If all this is possible, she can begin to enjoy the deeper relationship she truly yearns for.

The Fire woman easily attracts Earth and Water partners because of her strength and extrovert, sharp and dynamic personality. However, she may unconsciously project her own inner need for closeness and sensuality on to such types, and consequently feel claustrophobic and overwhelmed by the emotional contact of Water and the bodily intimacy of Earth. Projection is something we all do, whichever element we are, but Fire is probably more likely to project more insistently without even realizing that she's getting tangled up in the same old scenario again.

To ensure harmony in a relationship, the Fire woman must learn to go with the flow and not try to make others change to her pace. What she must also learn is that others have their own music to make, and if she could, for once slow down and listen, she might find the magic of other rhythms and desires that she may have been too afraid to look for within herself.

Sexual love for the Fire woman has to be passionate and she needs a lot of fantasy and excitement. Routine sex is definitely not for her, and she'll grow bored quickly if the man in her life runs out of romance, which is why she also needs friendship and mental stimulation.

The emotional intensity of Water can put out Fire's spark and Metal's drive can be a handy hook for Fire's dramatic need to be in control of her environment. Although she may be drawn to these types because they are so different on the surface, they are often the ones that cause her to fall into painful patterns in love.

In Feng Shui, Wood and Earth are possibly the best ways to harmonize Fire's environment in the home. The Fire lady produces a lot of energy, both in her heart and in her surroundings. This kind of energy is electric and too much Fire in the home can make her own inner Bagua energies crackle. Anger may rise to the surface with alarming repetition. For Fire, expressing anger is healthy and wise, as in any other element, but learning to channel anger is also important. In Feng Shui, if you balance the elements in your home, anger can be expressed positively and effectively. A volatile Fire woman must find a channel for this energy, otherwise her relationship may suffer.

Yang Fire

As Yang Fire you are doubly blessed with enthusiasm for sex, but dislike any kind of routine in your love-making. You want everything; to give and to take as much as you can within a physical relationship, but also to get out of it if it doesn't live up to your ideals. You can at times be jealous, egotistic and possessive. Most Yang Fire people want to dominate, so it's important for you to play a leading role in bed. Even if you have doubled up with another Yang Fire person you may need to learn to communicate your inner values. You may be good at listening to what's going on in your own head and vocalizing it, but not at listening to your partner. Get in touch with your likes and dislikes too and you may be surprised enough to tune into a different kind of love-making. Yang Fire can be pretty vulnerable underneath all that thrashing around, so if you're feeling emotional this may be the time to look hard at what love means to you. Commitment is a scary word, and you may often prefer to conquer and depart rather than commit and stay.

Slow down! This is probably the best way a Yang Fire lover can learn to channel that rampant energy.

Fantasy is an important part of sex for you. Having sex in public places, exhibitionism and initiation ceremonies conjure up all sorts of visual stimulation, and if your partner can cope with this kind of arousal then communicate your need for fantasizing together!

Yin Fire

You're not dissimilar to Yang Fire, but the subtle difference is you are more likely to play a strange mixture of one day a waiting game and the next an impatient one. The trouble arises because your energy doesn't get expressed so loudly; instead it can be repressed and drawn inwards and lead you to be so involved with yourself that everyone else seems insignificant. This is a kind of over-compensation for not being able to give off sexual steam! You need to share your anger and energy with your partner but you may find it difficult to open up in the bedtime scenarios with true passion.

What Yin Fire needs is more fun, more chances to let go and express inner tension, whether it's physical or in your head. Play games in bed, use mental analogies and don't assume that you have to have orgasms all night to prove anything! If you are feeling like sex and would rather dive straight in, take time to let romance come back into your life. Be creative with time. Learn to let go of the strong need to control others; sit back for once and let them come to you. If you find that your love life is beginning to settle into a routine – and Yin Fire really hates routine – opt for sex toys as well as fantasy sex. Because you may internalize all that energy have some Fire elements around your home. Moody candlelight and incense sticks are often excellent accessories to a new-found romance and may enhance more expressive love-making. For Yin Fire there is a tendency to expect too much from the partner and you may assume that being the centre of attention is enough in itself. However, Yin Fire needs to be flattered and loved and never compared to past lovers or relationships. You need to be handled with care!

Earth man

'The Earth and Ocean seem to sleep in one another's arms
. . . and dream of . . . woods, rocks, and all that we call
reality.'

The magical appeal of Earth element men relies on the fact that they never do the chasing or forcing in any relationship. Like the white rabbit in the magician's hat, the sensual Earth male gets pulled from his safe hideaway rather than making any attempt to leave it himself. Earth males play a 'catch me if you can' game. He is there to be discovered; it is not for him to do the discovering. Known for his fixed and dogmatic approach to life, he stays firmly rooted to the ground he knows, unless someone else comes along and literally cuts him down with one fell swoop. This is where Earth can get drawn and quartered more quickly than a log gets split in two! Because of his lack of vision he is not easily tempted into mad passionate love affairs, nor is he willing to change his easy-going and apparently placid way of life for anyone.

Earth's energy and sexual appetite are similar to his joy in the good things of life. Food, sensuality, baths, bed and sleep are as much a pleasure for the finely tuned senses of the Earth character as is making love in a field. This doesn't mean that he's not interested in sex – far from it. Earth oozes sexuality in a way that is hard to define. It's natural, and originates from the primeval core of Earth's body. He is sharply aware of his body, deeply fond of it, and can appear to be closer to nature than any other element. But in a way Earth is elusive. He has a longing for what he calls the spiritual or the ethereal. Because he is so down to earth, so involved in grounding everything in his life and love, he often becomes ecstatic about anyone who appears to be able to teach him the secrets of the spiritual world. But he faces losing the very person with whom he believed he could share a profound relationship solely because of his insistence that everything must be backed up by his senses.

The big plus point for Earth is his staying ability. Earth is probably the only element who grits his teeth and pretends there's nothing wrong, where most other elements would flee (not that this is always a saintly quality). Earth believes that if something is tangible, if it is there in front of his eyes and he can speak to it and hear it and feel it, then it is real, and that relationship must exist.

The Earth male is often magnetically captivated by Wood, who may be able to blow out candles, talk abstractly about life and love and play magical games. With any element we are drawn to those who appear to be different from ourselves, but Earth often gets hopelessly tangled up with the intellectual and breezy Wood type. Eventually he may find that he can't keep up with the speed and the mind-bending improvisations of this element, unless he learns to ride along with its capricious energy.

Earth will always be there for you, and he'll move heaven and earth if he can. His shoulder is ready to be cried on and his heart is open and compassionate, sincere and deeply loyal. He is a hedonist and his need for deeply erotic sex involves the body first and the mind second. Fantasy is not for him (although with Fire he can find new outlets for his imagination). Earth's sexuality must involve all the senses, and especially those of touch. He wants to be in the here and now, rather than lingering with past memories or future possibilities. Earth needs peace and tranquillity, not action and drama, and in love he needs to see tangible results for the effort he believes he puts into a relationship. However, for many of his partners there could be some doubt that he puts any effort into them at all! Earth will usually avoid conflict if he can, and his cynical and worldly attitude to love is highly infectious. He knows what relationships are about in reality, and he'll let you in on the secret if you care to tag along at his pace. Beauty is in the eye of the beholder for Earth, and if you show you love him by cooking him food, nurturing his body, massaging his ego and his back, or simply share the bathtub with him, you'll be astounded by the deep and sensuous side of this profoundly committed man.

He's not passionately incensed like Fire, not downright horny like Metal, not airy and abstract like Wood or emotionally responsive like Water, but he'll react to your every need with the knowledge of an erotic sensuality that quietly waits behind closed doors.

Changing his ways, his dreams (if he admits to having any) and his plans – he always has those – could be tricky and sometimes fatal. Change is not a word in his vocabulary, and he certainly won't want his partner to make changes too quickly in his home. Feng Shui may seem like a threat to his stability, so work carefully by planting the ideas in his head rather than trying to force him to move the bed or the cooker. (Both are essential paths to this man's soul.)

The main problem for Earth is that he does not know or does not remember how to play. In some ways he can seem worldly wise and old for his age, and may find it hard to connect to a partner who is light and frivolous, takes sex lightly and enjoys fun and games in her sexual expression. Earth is not a child for long, and may be tempted by childlike partners. He may need to compartmentalize his reality, and that can include his relationships. If his partner doesn't stick to the category she's been given, if she deviates from the truth as he sees it, she may well find that Earth grounds everything, including himself and the relationship, for ever.

Earth woman

'Go and catch a falling star,
Get with child a mandrake root
Tell me where all moonbeams are,
Or who cleft the devil's foot.'

The Earth woman will probably find the art of Feng Shui easier to understand than any other element. Without doubt she is highly sensual and in tune with her surroundings. Nature and her environment are part of her inner sense of being, and if she can't relate to the reality that is beauty in her eyes, she won't settle for second best. Harmony is important for the Earth woman, not only within her home but also within her relationships. On the surface she can appear cool, serene and sometimes aloof, but beneath this mask she is overtly sexual and intensely passionate in a most seductive way.

Earth women are eternally female. They are highly aware of themselves, their clothes, appearance and the richness of their style and values. Earth women connect to the physical sensuality of Aphrodite. We sometimes get the wrong impression of Aphrodite, viewing her as someone romantic and sublime. The paradox is that she symbolizes divine and sacred love as well as profane and forbidden love! You can see why Earth women have trouble sometimes wondering which direction to take when they meet someone who attracts them.

There is one pitfall that Earth woman must be careful of, and that is possession. She can be acutely possessive and jealous once she has decided the object of her desire is worthy of her intense physical involvement. She is certainly not promiscuous, but she has an instinctive reaction to a man who sends shivers down her spine, so if she's alone and waiting (because Earth women, like Earth men, don't hunt their prey) and the right smile or the right touch activates her need for physical closeness, she won't hesitate in becoming the seductress herself. However, Earth needs to nourish others and in doing so can become overbearing and possessive. It's all right for Earth to adore her lover or her partner, but not OK for anyone else to do so. She may alienate his family or his workmates in order to keep him to herself. Less worryingly, she may collect many objects of beauty in her home, cook well and be delightful in any company. Underneath this is a desperate need for security, and she truly believes that owning the things she loves will provide her with that sense of safety.

For Earth, the greatest test of her love is truly to let go of her partner, in such a way that they both have their space and their freedom. If Earth can understand that space doesn't necessarily mean danger and that letting someone be who they are doesn't mean that she won't be herself any more, she may find that her deep physical love can find its own mode of expression too.

The Earth woman seldom has affairs or one-night stands when she is sure about the man she loves. She is monogamous and sees her partner as a permanent fixture in her life. Her home will express the key elements of her need for security. Change is not easy for her to deal with, especially in a relationship.

The Earth woman might do well to take a few risks occasionally. She could learn a lot through a Fire partner, and often this combination, although not always smooth, can work extremely well. Fire has the ability to explode an Earth woman's dignity and grace with his directness and passion, and she'll never forget the feeling of power it gives her. Sex to the Earth woman is simple; a basic instinct, good gutsy sex which relies on body awareness rather than complicated gymnastics. The ground, or the earth, is where lightning conductors direct huge charges of energy from the sky, and in a way the Earth woman is always a lightning conductor for other people's passions, heartaches, dreams and anger. Earth needs warmth and affection, gentleness and nurturing. She gives it out so easily but usually expects something in return. She needs to learn to trust givingness as an inner resource that asks for no feedback.

The Earth woman may for a while enjoy dissolving in the ever-changing emotional expressions of Water, but could find it increasingly hard to accept that element's changes and flexibility. Earth needs time, and Water people create their own timetable, however fast or slow they desire it. With Wood, Earth can learn to focus on the whole rather than just on the self. Wood people are more universal in their loving than Earth, who is essentially personal in her desire. With Metal, the Earth woman may find the strength and resolve of this element complements her own need for security, for Metal has the intuition and the foresight to know what Earth really and truly desires.

Yang Earth

Beyond love there is an internal energy that keeps the steady determination of Yang Earth's longing for comfort and stability alive. The usually passive Earth personality here becomes extroverted and at times impatient. If you find you need to let off steam, the time to do so is when you begin to sense the changes occurring in your body, as Earth always responds best to physical indicators. Your powerful sexuality means you are ready to throw yourself into a deep physical bond once you are sure that your senses are telling you to go for it. One of the subtle nuances of Yang Earth energy is that you may unconsciously identify with whoever you are with. In other words if your partner is brash, bold and inventive, you may find this rubs off on you, and your normal urge for basic sex may be displaced by the antics of a gymnast! Your Yang Earth energy also expresses itself by creating love around your partner, rather than attending to your own needs and values first. What you yourself value in love and life is worth investigating, otherwise you may find that you are making love under the cloak of your partner's imagination. Your generosity may mean you lose sight of your own goals within any physical set-up. Remember, you need time – loads of it; body contact – tons of it; pleasure rather than pure sexual gratification, and you need a reminder that for you sex equals love. If you cannot express these things easily to your partner and you find you are always willing to please rather than asking for what pleases you, take a few more risks in communicating – even if it's a simple 'How about tickling my toes?'

Yin Earth

Discretion is essential for the Yin Earth sexuality. The more discreet and the more hidden the display of physical desire, the more Yin Earth will take comfort in the security of believing they are still backstage. Waiting in the wings to walk on in a non-speaking part is preferable to being in the limelight. Yin Earth prefers to play timidly at first, but you will probably find out eventually that you have strong sexual instincts that cannot be ignored. However, because you fear rejection you may find yourself preferring casual relationships in the knowledge that you're less likely to get hurt if things go wrong. This is Earth's basic survival instinct getting out of hand! Yin Earth doesn't easily take the initiative, but can be quite subversive if involved in a clandestine relationship – because it's safer that way.

Yin Earth has a deeply sensual hunger, and oral sex is one of the most powerful stimulations for your sexual urgency. You must express your need for comfort and nurturing, however basic an instinct this may appear to others. Yin Earth's fear of rejection is powerful, but the internalizing of your basic instincts can only detract from the physical and sensual fulfilment you could achieve if you allowed yourself to go out on a limb and be unpredictable. The main thing for Yin Earth to remember is to get in touch with your body and enjoy it.

Metal man

'Gold he wore against his brow;
chain-mail across his heart ... '

To be so sure of yourself, so certain that you are right and convinced others will believe this too, can seem to most of us an attainment hardly to be desired. But the Metal male is not only besotted with his sense of self, but absolutely determined to prove himself to those around him. It's not that Metal is particularly arrogant. He is simply so convinced of his own rightness, his own honour and his own strength in handling people and situations that anyone with whom he has a relationship will inevitably be impressed too.

Metal symbolizes wealth and prosperity in the elemental cycle, and Metal types are coincidentally the most ambitious, often the most ruthless and usually the most successful on the path to excellence in any field. However, the problem for Metal man is that finding the ultimate treasure trove doesn't always bring with it the happiness he assumed it should.

It is the same within relationships. The biggest hurdle a Metal man has to cross is the fact that in dealing with relationships he has to stop and listen. Metal assumes that his chosen partner – and he usually does the choosing – will respond to his every whim. It's easy for this steady and inflexible man to set himself up as the breadwinner, the charmer, the lover and the father figure without hesitation. On the surface he may seem like a lucky find to the woman who can get close enough to him, but the Metal man has not only a chain-mail conviction, but also a chain-mail heart.

What Metal loves is to feel in control because to him this is power. Power is mentally written on Metal's brow, and when romance comes knocking at their door, they will use their coolest, most subtle and, ironically, most invasive approach to get the relationship moving in the direction they want it to go. Being such a self-evolved and independent type means this chunk of Metal is usually single-minded about women! This is a definite plus to any relationship. He is unlikely to stray once he's truly involved in a relationship that can maintain his initial hunch about the woman of his choice. However, there may be times when Metal withdraws into solitary moods. Then he is prone to self-criticism, self-doubt and much introspection. Metal is hard to be with when he's in one of these phases and is usually best left well alone. In a way, these periods of depression are necessary for him to regenerate his strength in readiness to take over from where he left off.

Ambition is an important aspect of Metal's hunger for power, and you may find a Metal man will drop you for his career if a conflict arises. His sense of independence and of excellence makes Metal incredibly dedicated to his own path in life, and if a partner comes along who doesn't have the same kind of route mapped out, a Metal man might well let you know where to find the exit door.

Metal assumes he will never fail in a relationship. If a woman ever walks out on him, he is quite capable of transforming his attitude to the relationship – almost as if he meant it to happen. Strangely he often does. This man will sometimes stop at nothing until he has destroyed the very relationship that he believes he created. This is Metal 'gone wrong' if you like, the type who suffers from delusions of power, is out for himself alone and refuses to rely on anyone else for emotional support. And there are a few of them about!

In some ways Metal is impregnable. His strength and serious reflection on life and love can make him seem cold, unfeeling and unloving. He is, however, highly intuitive, has superb staying powers where others would crack up, and a nerve that can take your breath away. Endurance is a word that in Metal's vocabulary means attaining his goals. In physical relationships the Metal man may set out slowly, romance sparking his interest at first, as long as it is followed by some kind of intellectual stimulation. There are also Metal men who are so solitary that a quick fling or a one-night stand will mean little to them, but remember, their performance will be superb.

Metal's intuition means he will usually know what turns his partner on before they've even made love. And Metal, although at first he seems calculating, experienced and worldly wise in the bedroom, may soften with time to become a truly warm and passionate lover. However, sex to this man is a powerful pleasure and also a form of self-indulgence. Partners must be prepared for times when Metal may seem to be thinking only of himself.

In some ways the serious mask Metal wears in his love life serves only to hide the lonely body behind it. Metal can be happy alone, but with the kind of woman who both respects and honours his enterprise and self-possession, Metal can be a faithful and loyal partner. Integrity is the link that holds his chain-mail together.

Metal does best with Earth, and can feel in control with the ebb and flow of Water. In some ways the adaptability and restlessness of Water is something that Metal needs to integrate into his life so that he can learn that relationships are more than an iron chain clanking around his heart. With Fire he may feel like hot Metal, ready to turn white, ghosted out of his own autonomy! The almost childlike dynamism of Fire is very different to the motivation and conviction of Metal, and although opposites attract – leading to some of the most erotic relationships – there may well come a time when Fire grows weary of Metal's need for solitude, and Metal becomes blackened by the heat of Fire's quest for fun.

Wood, on the other hand, may be stripped of her universal and social functions and find it hard to live with someone who is so deeply enmeshed in themselves. For Metal the charm of Wood may wear thin when he realizes that his own importance in the relationship is insignificant compared to the altruistic values that inspire Wood.

The greatest test for the Metal man, like the tin man

in the Wizard of Oz, is to find his heart. For this lonely and autonomous soul really does have one!

Metal woman

'Your holy delicate white hands
Shall girdle me with steel.'

The steely eyes of the Metal woman will fix on a man who is able to offer her independence, within a conventional (in her eyes) and honest relationship where she can trust without fear. However, this woman will need to be the boss both physically and emotionally.

'Magnetic' is a word that partners, lovers and even friends will use about her with varying degrees of feeling. One thing is clear, she makes sparks fly whether by fascinating or frightening potential suitors! Devastation is often a theme in her relationships, for if a Metal woman doesn't team up with someone who can offer her solidity and respect, yet still allow her to indulge her wildest dreams, she may destroy that partnership in cold blood. Like her Metal male counterpart, the Metal woman is fascinated by sexuality and the power it brings. This doesn't mean she is a beast of the night, but that she needs to enjoy the dangers and the mystery of intimate and erotic sexual relationships. But for all the danger, she is unlikely to sleep around. First, she is possessive and a loner, and second, she will feel great waves of guilt if her behaviour becomes too extreme.

Competitive and ambitious, the Metal woman may find herself in a lonely life and career where relationships are difficult to enjoy. But this seriousness is not her only hindrance to a close partnership. With such a strong need to survive, there is an iron bar that shuts out many who would dare to come closer. It's OK for Metal to penetrate and invade a lover's spirit, but not for him to attempt to touch hers!

A Metal woman has difficulty in expressing her anger, and this can have an unfortunate effect on those who would like to be more involved in her life. Anger has a way of manifesting itself in those around her, and a partner may have to carry her rage on her behalf.

The Metal woman is a born climber so she will always succeed in any walk of life in which she feels comfortable. Excellence and integrity are essential to her happiness, so if a partner doesn't have either she may well dump him. She wants status and prestige, love and honour, to go together in one person. But she rarely finds the perfect combination. This is why she prefers to be alone (even though she feels acutely lonely) and finds it easier to live an independent and self-reliant life because her fear of losing in love is greater than her belief that she can find her ideal. She compensates by over-achieving in other areas of life, in her business pursuits, her career, her appearance and her apparent hardness. However, if Metal cannot crumble, it can melt, a notion of which she is too painfully aware. Communication is not a high priority on her list, and sometimes she may prefer to listen to music and dance the night away rather than settle down for an intimate chat with a Wood element, or a passionate argument with Fire. She frequently falls in love with these potent elemental types. They are both good hooks for her apparent lack of abstraction or ability to take risks, and the Metal woman will submit to the provocative optimism of Fire and the freedom of Wood.

Unlike does attract unlike. If Fire allows Metal to enjoy her own autonomy and listens for a change to her need for a highly erotic relationship, these different elements could learn to complement each other. Sexually she can play both the seducer and the seduced. This is part of her strong emphasis on independence as a value. If she can lead, she will be able to leave; if she follows she may be able to merge so quickly into another's arms that she won't have time for intimate conversation. Like Wood she fears intimacy but for different reasons. Metal's determination to infiltrate another's heart often turns into a more torrid affair than she can handle – which is why, when a close and binding relationship results from a fun moment, she will feel her own autonomy is threatened. Glamour, money and power go hand in hand for this lady, sometimes at the cost of her sexual relationships. But for all her vanity, for all her strong survival instinct, she has great anxieties. If she could learn to express these, she might achieve a more harmonious lifestyle and a more relaxed relationship with the world. Keeping her distance may seem her safest option on the road to tranquillity. But for the Metal woman, letting go and letting herself love and laugh could release her from her fears. It may be that she needs Water's specific fluidity and sensitivity to give her the chance to look at life from the outside of her metal cage, rather than from behind those steely bars.

With a Metal man she may lock swords and find herself reflected in his eyes. This is often a test of her own strength and courage and one which can prove to be irresistible and insatiable. However, it may be that it is only the solid and long-lasting integrity of Earth which can sustain a relationship with this highly magnetic and soulful woman.

Earth has the ability to live in the here and now and ground the experience of love, a reality which Metal woman truly needs.

Yang Metal

Friction, whether physical or mental, is essential to Yang Metal's sexual expression. Sparks fly for Yang Metal because, while maintaining your sense of autonomy, you are likely to seek out variety to test your powerful urges within a sexual relationship. When you succeed in expressing yourself you will feel 'on top' for a while, and in some cases you may go after impossible relationships, or sexually impossible entanglements, just to prove your independence. You have to be in charge of the relationship, but you may find that few people can satisfy your hunger for sexual fulfilment. The magnetism you exude is exciting rather than welcoming.

Leading your partner into the realms of the unknown could be a big turn-on. When physically aroused you like taking the lead; which is the most positive way to feel really close to the partner of your choice. Dedication to your own bed and what goes on in it is one thing, but you will probably never commit yourself totally to someone else's bed unless it can offer you access to eternal Eros.

The dilemma for Yang Metal is that although you can instigate inspirational sex in others, your own torrid energies cause friction for you. Honesty is your ally; if you really want to explore taboo sex or exotic themes, communicate your desires to your partner. Astute you may be, but learn that others don't always share your tastes or your energy!

Yin Metal

Sexual longing for Yin Metal is almost as enjoyable as sexual completion. The sensitive and in-tune Yin Metal radiates desire towards a possible lover. Yet like a metal detector on the beach, you can pick up the energy around you, the smallest vibration, the minutest electrical charge. So aware, so electric is your sensory system that sometimes Yin Metal has difficulty in being out there in the big wide world, particularly one full of rampant passion and your own unnerving energy.

As Yin Metal you may face the problem of being ultra secretive; close communication, whether across a bar table or the pillow, is nil. Self-reliance apart, you fear dependency on a partner for sexual fulfilment, and you may be the one who calls it a day.

Love is connected with a deep sexual need for Yin Metal but your sexuality needs to be nurtured by romance and honesty. You need deeply erotic experiences but you must be careful of the temptation to go looking for sexual relationships that have no meaning for you. Yin Metal thrives on a rich and intense sex life because Sex *is* love to Yin Metal, and however hard you find it to subdue your need for physical control, you may discover that allowing others to make sexual decisions or seize the initiative is the route towards inner confidence.

Water man

'The allure of something so unattainable was what fascinated and held him caught for a second, in a web of his own making.'

Water males are usually drawn to very beautiful and very feminine women, and are easily infatuated by physical appearance. What Water men think they see, or rather the ideal from which they find it hard to detach themselves, is often the cause of their falling in love more frequently than any other element. Although Fire has a habit of rushing blindly into a relationship, he knows that he is doing it. Water gets caught in the current before he even thinks about it.

The Water man has a reputation for inconsistency and a gullible attitude when it comes to socializing. Water males are easily led astray by wine, women and song. It is in their nature to be gregarious, to enjoy life and love in a light and transient way, for their hearts are so open to the feelings of those around them and their minds and bodies are so in tune with the world and its vibrations that they walk around like sponges soaking up everyone else's problems, without knowing whether they have any of their own.

The Water man must learn that he has feelings too, for although he may shrug his shoulders and prefer to offer you advice, his resistance to his own feelings is the reason he seems like a ship passing in the night. There is a state of partial eclipse that the Water male lives in, when love encounters are thrown in his path. He may escape into shadowland and the deeper waters of his own dreams rather than face the reality of a relationship if it does not live up to his ideal.

Yet for all his unpredictable and unfocused ways the Water male is versatile, spontaneous and ready for any sexual or mental challenge. He lives on a cloud. The bright flames of Fire's passion and the deeply erotic Metal sexuality are a rarity in his love life. He is a catalyst for communication.

He plays mental gymnastics in bed, and games that don't involve his heart. He'll prefer to laugh over a few bottles of wine than get involved in heavy emotional scenes. Conflict and chaos are not for him. He may move through his new lover's life like a shooting star – and if he does manage to remain a more permanent fixture he certainly won't make any promises about tomorrow, let alone next week!

The sadness is that Water men never really let you into their emotional space. They may seem glamorous and charming, persuasive and intuitive, but their emotional boundaries are firmly defined and they let few people cross the line. Water males have trouble knowing what love is, because what they imagine to be love is often just a fantasy. No one ever seems to live up to the Water male's expectations, and his constant need for change means that he may never make his bed or lie in it.

The Water man has an extraordinary ability to act out all kinds of lovers imaginable. This role playing means he doesn't have to be truly himself, and he doesn't want to know who he is anyway. It's safer to be the receptor of everyone else's feelings rather than to do any giving. This is one of the difficulties with falling in love with a Water man: they give away very little of themselves.

However, they have an innate and often unconscious fear of loneliness, and you won't find Water males living alone for long. That doesn't mean they seek a permanent partner. They are likely to have a variety of girlfriends with no commitment to anyone in particular, or perhaps share a house or flat with another male friend. The Water man thrives on company because he prefers to keep moving, to keep changing his mask and to explore new experiences rather than stand in the fog of the tried and tested. Sexually he's fun and light-hearted, but his preference for romantic encounters may mean he gets involved with Fire too often for his own good. The inconsistency of Water will exasperate Fire and a relationship with Earth can prove equally tense. Water's flexible nature may bend too many of Earth's strong values and fixed perceptions of how love should be. Bending the rules is something Water does naturally, but Earth may have trouble sharing yet another adventure in wonderland.

Both Metal and Wood can add the missing ingredients of integrity and self-esteem, or altruism and freedom, for Water to enjoy himself without anxiety. It's a high price to pay, but Water can be a lost boy if he doesn't find someone who knows that he feels his way through relationships as if they were dark halls filled with ghosts and possible traps. The light at the end of the tunnel is there, but he needs an unusual and perceptive guide.

Water woman

'The time and my intents are savage wild,
More fierce . . . than empty tigers or the roaring sea.'

Amber is rare and was highly valued by ancient civilizations. The mythical provider of Amber has always been a goddess of the sea. This is where the Water woman is best represented, both by her fluidity and changeability and by her rare ethereal quality, at times elusive and difficult to grasp – rather like Amber.

Her gregarious and seemingly capricious nature may sparkle at parties, enticing many men and infuriating many women. In a way she appears to be what she least wants to be. The Water-dominated woman has a difficult time convincing anyone that she can be loyal and consistent for all her charm and wit. She is at the mercy of the Moon, just like the tides of the ocean. Her sensitivity to the world around her is so intense that she can paint portraits of an ex-lover within her own head and then project those pictures on to every other man she meets after he has gone. To be invaded by so many vibrations means that love is a difficult game for her to play, and yet she longs to enjoy it for what it is, however high the stakes.

This may be why the Water woman seems to have many different relationships and is likely to get involved with the wrong types, simply because she is uncertain of what love is. Romance is high on her agenda, as is sexual love. But her noncommittal approach at the beginning of a relationship may swing between assuming her new-found lover to be the man of her dreams and accepting the transiency of such a relationship. Because of this inability to know what she truly feels, the Water woman may swim against many tides. If she could learn to receive for herself alone, to know her own feelings as separate from those of others, then she could involve herself in a more permanent and lasting relationship. This is what she wants, but not often what she gets.

Water woman's talent for communication can lead her into many tricky situations. She has the knack of talking her way out of anything, especially if she comes across an opposite type like Fire, whom she is certain to enrage with her unfocused lifestyle. Yet it is for her gentle and beguiling appearance that men will chase her in the hope of capturing her elusive and airy heart. The paradox of this woman is that although she enjoys the chase, gets a giggle out of playing at seduction and romance, she is also liable to change her mind and refuse to be part of the action at all. This is the duality of the Water woman, nomadic but in need of permanence, unpredictable but still able to hook into her lover's spirit and hold him beside her. To be so vulnerable may seem a weakness, and yet in her relationships this can sometimes be her greatest ally and strength. If she finds a man who protects and nourishes her and allows her enough rope to feel she has not committed her whole self, she is more likely to remain a permanent fixture.

Water women need to experience many different relationships to discover who they truly are. They try on different partners – rather as other women try on different clothes – to see which suits them best. These experiments make her feel more 'real'. Yet Water is sure she wants *one* relationship, and one in which she can function without feeling committed or tied down. This is the difficulty she always faces, and which poses a big problem for anyone with whom she becomes involved. Her unsettling and sometimes neurotic behaviour seems at odds with her desire for the man she loves. But sustaining a relationship is hard for Water unless she gets an awful lot of variety in a one-to-one partnership, or can swim away from it and back again when she chooses. This is, of course, a hard lesson in sexual swimming for any partner.

Avoiding confrontations is essential for the Water woman. Not only will she deny that a conflict may have arisen, but she will go out of her way to escape a scene. The disharmony of life is something she finds hard to deal with.

Earth may find her frustrating, not only because of her

changeability and unfocused mind, but also because she won't stay around for long if Earth reverts to being possessive and tenacious. The problem for Water is that she idealizes every man she meets, sees only what she wants to see, and then when he doesn't live up to her vision she either does a disappearing act or becomes so flirtatious that he leaves her. Once involved in a relationship Water woman needs much sexual variety, and a lot of fun and light-hearted play. Sex becomes a bore for her if it's not channelled into an amusing pastime. Physical expression has to be romantic, imaginative and escapist.

The experimental and extrovert Wood may hold her attention longer than any other element. Metal's torrid and intense magnetic appeal will lure her into a romantic trance, and her own special charm is equally challenging and provocative to Metal. But her mutability and inconsistency may prove incompatible with the ego of Fire and the possessiveness of Earth. Like the goddess who brings Amber from the sea, she may disappear on the tide as easily as she came.

Yang Water

The archetypal quality of Yang Water's sexual expression is the search for as many new experiences within a relationship as possible. Yang Water's quest is also about giving oneself too quickly and getting as much as possible, whether by force or by subtly undermining their partner or lover's intent. The big problem for Yang Water is the tendency never to give anything in return. As they soak up the energy of the relationship so easily, and instantly reflect the feelings of their lover, there may come a time when the genuine and the pretend begin to confuse even them.

Activity and change are necessary to keep the energy levels of this highly gregarious sexuality channelled positively. It is essential that you can tune your mind, as well as your body, towards sexual happiness. Mental stimulation is as important as physical, and you will find it hard to enjoy sexual love without a partner who can satisfy your inner search for yourself. Respecting someone else's mind means you will relax in a sexual encounter, otherwise you'll hunger for more. The phases in your life where you may meet and form many casual attachments are a reflection of this.

The idea of sexual ecstasy may be more erotic than the sexual act itself to you! Communication and mental eroticism may be the key to keeping you attuned to one partner in the long term. You may find erotic phone calls, long-distance love or sex while travelling inspirational. But finding the ideal partner is a long and difficult road because Yang Water doesn't have the time to check out what is really under the bedclothes. Experience is everything to Yang Water, and finding a partner who can enjoy the lighter side of sexuality and provide intellectual variety is their pathway to a more challenging and positive sexual identity.

Yin Water

The fluidity and tranquillity of Water is best expressed in calm, serene love-making. Yin Water's sexuality is an elusive and secretive thing which at times may seem far removed from more earthly and bodily types. But Yin Water's desire is geared towards responsive tactics. Yin Water moves with whoever they are with, and they are like mirrors to their partner's own instincts and needs, sometimes to the extent of forgetting their own.

Yin Water takes time to awaken to a new lover or partner, yet often seeks variety quietly and dangerously. In a way you depend on intrigue or cloak-and-dagger relationships although this can bring you difficulties, conflicts and painful love. You may also find that aesthetics are a high priority in your choice of partner – pretty men, pretty women, musicians, poets and visionaries rather than rough and fast-living, money-grabbing types. Yin Water has more patience than Yang Water and therefore you can be more consistent in your relationships. Your sensual appetite is hungry but it is never predictable or part of a routine. You can be both demanding and egotistic on the mental level, yet ambivalent when it comes to making a commitment. This is the dual nature of Water; the ebbs and flow of your sexual dynamics are never entirely stilled by your partner. Fantasy is a big part of Yin Water's sexuality. If your partner can listen and realize that the mystery and imagination deeply embedded in your sexual energy must be expressed, perhaps you can begin to experience the dynamite exchange that you so long for. Desire and fantasy can then merge to transform your sexuality into something tangible, if only you allow the alchemy to take place.

Wood man

'I'm a lumberjack and I'm OK . . . '

A relationship that is deeply emotive, rich in feeling or intimate to the point of virtual-twinning is not for the Wood man. This is a male who finds warmth and closeness difficult, although he seeks out quality and perfection in every woman he meets. The Wood male will analyse his own sexual performance as well as his partner's with the same interest and meticulous attention to detail he would use if he were analysing his weekly petrol receipts. The truth is that Wood men don't really need anyone else in their lives. They often panic about their lack of passion and then devote oodles of time to worrying about it. Fretting about life is one of their big inconsistencies.

Wood men want to incorporate relationships into one big universal love. They find it hard to accept the intimacy of a marriage or partnership that involves exclusivity. Their need is for freedom of self, but above all freedom for everyone.

Wood males are radical in relationships, and prefer to have acquaintances rather than partners; lovers rather than wives. However, this sophisticated man encounters many cul-de-sacs because he expects everyone else to share his humanitarian and idealistic vision of love. He can seem alluring and highly sociable – almost too sociable as he'll chat to many women and won't single anyone out unless they are his intellectual equal. He tends to stay friends with past partners or girlfriends and may well invite X round for a drink to meet his new amour, thinking that they should be the best of friends too. After all, they both fell for him, didn't they?

This altruism, which may work extremely well for Wood in the wider world, doesn't often work that well in his relationships. Most of the partners he meets are those whose values aren't his, simply because most people are more concerned about the exclusivity of a one-to-one relationship.

There may be radical and unconventional partners around, but even today the majority of women would prefer not to share their man with every ex-girlfriend or lover whenever he chooses.

Being a sexual egalitarian means that he is skilfully experienced in the art of love-making. His passion is one of experimentation rather than earthy sensuality. He fears intimacy, and for Wood a sexual relationship means avoiding that closeness. He'd be willing to agree that sex is a process involving two bodies and two needs, and an intellectual lesson in co-operation and seduction! But his experience tells all. He can be liberal with his own needs and highly aware of his partner's. As long as he can maintain his freedom and a sense of not belonging to anyone, he may be able to focus on one partnership for the good of the whole. However, his philosophy is such that if you try to possess him, he will flee, and if you give him loose reins he may stray anyway. The irony is that he can become frustrated and opinionated about a relationship if it doesn't go according to his strategy. Wood's ego is strongly focused on the reality of a relationship and how he can organize and direct it. He may find that Water partners stimulate his need to communicate – for he has a serious problem on a one-to-one level here – and Metal may remind him of the autonomy that he expects for society, but tends to forget for the individual. However much he chats about the goals of mankind and the schemes for how to get on in life, which he is superbly able to orchestrate, his perception is tunnel-visioned. His chit-chat is about connections and abstractions, rather than feelings and needs.

The paradox of Wood is that he wants to be everyone's friend, everyone's guru, and yet stick to his own specific lifestyle. He loves to see others progress, for people to grow, change their lovers, change their lifestyle, but his personal aim is to avoid doing so himself! Checking out the inner workings of a possible new relationship is essential for him. This is because he needs to be absolutely sure that the object of his desire is tough enough mentally to cope with his experimental mind. Love is impersonal to the Wood male. He takes it from others and hands it out with the same degree of fairness to everyone. In a way he *trades* in love, rather than falls in love, so his partner of the moment had better remember never to think she's someone special!

Being friends and sharing his ideals and need for freedom are more important to Wood than a monogamous relationship. Sex comes second to the Wood male – sure, he'll enjoy it and he'll play an excellent part at every performance, but somehow the lure of the big wide world motivates him far more than sitting tight with one woman in suburbia. This is a man of action, of achievement and of big schemes. He is the diplomat in love and sex, and he can handle most kinds of relationship with a detached and undemanding air. Flying high with him could be a trip to the stars and back but he needs to learn to relate, in the truest sense of the word. The Wood man is probably the most ambiguous of the elements in that he searches desperately to find and to know himself, but it is only through others, through the reflection in the mirror, that he can begin to understand who he really is.

Wood woman

'And Freedom rear'd in that august sunrise
Her beautiful bold brow.'

Honesty, beauty and truth are at least three of the mental ideals that the Wood woman aspires to. She is attractive, gregarious and articulate, and has a strong sense of spirit and independence. In fact because she is so freedom-loving she often goes out of her way to avoid ever making a commitment or a promise that would mean she's trapped. Wood hates to reject anything or anyone, because it may mean losing out on an experience that could be in line with her ideal.

Aesthetic principles play a big part in the way she begins relationships. She is particularly drawn to good looks, and can fall instantly in love with the right kind of face. This also leads her to make a habit of falling for the wrong type of man.

Falling in love with love is easy. Although she appears cool and poised on the surface, the French polish act is only a fine veneer for her vulnerability – the part that fears loneliness and yet fears intimacy. For all her independence and love of the wild side, she wants to be held and nurtured; for all her big ambitions, humanitarian ideals and sophisticated lifestyle, she has a fragile heart that seeks love and yet fears its closeness.

Wood women have a problem in communicating their needs both physical and emotional. Mind you, Wood woman can talk her way in and out of any debate, and make extrovert and broad-minded statements to state her case in business or pleasurable pursuits without a hint of anxiety. But there is something rather too liberal and ambivalent about her connection with others when confronted with the very personal!

She would probably find the changeability of Water men inspiring as this would enable her to stay free from too intense a relationship and still maintain an intellectual connection. Her personal space is hers, and there are few times in her life when she'll let anyone in to share it.

The Wood woman is never possessive and hates to be possessed. She prefers to lead an unconventional lifestyle and might be more interested in gathering her vast circle of friends together on a night out, rather than one man and his hang-ups. Often, however, she refuses to listen to others and will stubbornly persist in her awkward views simply for the sake of it!

What unbends a Wood woman is a relationship with someone who can allow her to feel free and untrapped. Her vision is practical, common-sensical and filled with intellectual knowledge. Cages are for those who submit! This woman likes to feel in control, to hold the power in her own hands. Because she is so convinced of her goals in life, it can be hard for her to find a deep inner meaning in a relationship, so she turns it into an intellectual exercise. Love is something which happens in her head rather than in her heart.

Too much passion implies commitment and intensity, and to a Wood woman both are frightening. She enjoys sex and physical contact as a pleasurable activity, but she prefers men who aren't slushy or sentimental. She needs someone who can keep their distance and still be there for her as a friend. That's why Metal and Water are both suited to this partnership. Fire she finds intensely proud but endlessly provocative; Earth too close, and over-affectionate. She will dig deeply into her Metal partner's head, winkle out all his intentions and scan him for signs of wear and tear from ex-lovers. She admires perfection in a guy! Genuine independence is what turns her on, as well as experimenting with new ideas and the more obscure games of sophisticated sexuality. A Metal partner could be prepared to respect her freedom and her invention. Equality is the most important value for the Wood woman and if Water can provide the romance and allow her to flow freely among her own ideals, there is a chance that she'll hang out with him longer than most.

Wood women live better alone than with a partner and spend much of their lives independently succeeding in careers rather than in motherhood. If they are scattered in their friendships, it's because it's safer to have an open house, and if they are liberal in their love-making it is because they have never found anyone to match their high ideals and principles. Wood lives and loves well in the current energies of society and changing roles. But the Wood woman is still a woman, even though that may be harder for her than any other element. To be responsive is not a problem. Seduction is an art she can share – but only if she finds a partner who won't try to possess her but will give her the freedom she so desperately needs.

Yang Wood

Agility, both intellectual and physical, are prime requisites for what Yang Wood seeks in a partner. Expressing your own creative pursuit of pleasure means you need more than just the sexual act to satisfy you. Romance in the head and in the body are equally important. The early games and inter-action of two people finding out about each other are often more exciting and challenging than a relationship that has reached a static compromise. As aesthetics come into Yang Wood's own expression, you may be attracted to beauty and need to feel beautiful yourself. Independence is prominently marked in Yang Wood people, so make sure that your part-ner or chosen lover understands your need for freedom both sexually and in a partnership. This doesn't mean you have to be promiscuous or that you want to be. What freedom means to Yang Wood is never having to feel restricted or held back from a sexual direction which attracts you.

The fear of being devoured emotionally by your lover or partner may mean you have to take control and indulge in your chosen sexual adventures, rather than tagging along in the wake of anyone else's ideas. In that way you can avoid emotional entanglements. The more detached and the more scattered your sexual preferences, the easier it is for you to co-operate with others. You may be fascinated by all kinds of sexual antics and use this to hide your fear of intimacy. The more outrageous and spirited the physical contact, the easier it is to feel comfortable! If you express your fears, sexu-ality can become a more relaxed and fulfilling experience.

Yin Wood

If you are Yin Wood you may find that spreading the butter too thin means that you miss out on a more indulgent sex life! Giving and generosity is Yin Wood's way of being in control. Placating everyone's needs, sharing yourself equally or romancing to an excess may mean you lose out on what you truly value in a sexual relationship. This over-diplomatic attempt at finding an idealistic relationship means you'll meet many who feel they can trust you. Yet the result of always feeding the world and never taking anything from it may be that you miss out on getting to know yourself. Falling in love or having an intimate physical relationship may seem like an awful lot of trouble to go to, but if you're Yin Wood you need to learn to let go for once, to take a risk. Don't always assume you know what the outcome will be! Cookbook sex isn't the answer, but establishing what makes you feel good is. Taking risks can be quite frightening, but it's the only way you'll ever move closer to another person and still maintain your independence. You can learn through your own curiosity and really enjoy your sexual expression if you try to release your mind from taking over every time you are involved in a sexual embrace. Your mind is powerful: use it well but don't allow it to judge you, your partner, the sexual performance or your feelings.

Full Circle

Love means different things to each of us, and has a profound and magical effect on us all. Love has an energy all of its own, for it is the most powerful and compelling of human emotions.

What this book has sought to do is to give you insight into your own needs, whether they are sexual, material, emotional or intellectual. It has, perhaps, also given you a better understanding of what this thing called love really is, and how the simple art of Wind and Water can help balance and harmonize your relationships.

Feng Shui works with invisible patterns of energy that are everywhere around us and inside us. But however much you play with the environment, unless you are working simultaneously on the you within, happiness cannot arrive of its own accord. The Feng Shui energy, the Ch'i, is mysterious, untouchable and invisible, but if you trust in the universe and its workings, and you trust in your heart and learn to understand who you really are, maybe you'll glimpse what this mystery is all about.

To untangle the web in our own home and our own inner life is to follow just one silken strand of that bigger thread that weaves its way through time and universal magic.

Ah, Love! Could thou and I with fate conspire
To grasp this sorry scheme of things entire,
Would not we shatter it to bits – and then
Re-mould it nearer to the heart's desire?
(*Rubáiyát of Omar Khayyám*)

Index